FINDING
RESILIENCE

FINDING RESILIENCE

Lessons Learned from Getting
Lost in the Borneo Jungle

STEVE CAMKIN

With Contributions by
MUKHTAR MAKUSSARA

LUMINARE PRESS

WWW.LUMINAREPRESS.COM

Luminare Press
442 Charnelton St.
Eugene, OR 97401
www.luminarepress.com

LCCN: 2021915804
ISBN: 978-1-64388-769-2

CONTENTS

1

LOST

*"Some beautiful paths can't be discovered
without getting lost."*

EROL OZAN

"AUSTRALIAN WHO MYSTERIOUSLY VANISHED IN AN INDONESIAN JUNGLE IS MIRACULOUSLY FOUND A WEEK LATER."

That was the headline in the UK Daily Mail. That evening the story also aired on several television stations in Australia. The headline actually understated how long Mukhtar and I had just spent lost in the Borneo jungle.

I had been able to contact my family and friends just a few hours before the news broadcasts to tell them I was out of the Borneo jungle after being "lost" for 14 days. If I had not reached them then the T.V. broadcasts would have been the first time they would have learned of my situation.

The story, as published, included some exaggeration. Newspaper reports described us as "emaciated" (I lost about 15-20 lbs.), in "very weak condition", in "a bad way" and "left with limited logistics". Reports claimed we "were looked over by medical staff". However, that did not happen; it was not necessary. Still, we had been out of contact for 14 days, with little to no food. We were not certain of our exact location for 11 of those days. During some of those 11 days, we knew we were heading in the right direction. Porters from Apauping reported us overdue when they trekked to our planned meeting point in the jungle and could not locate us. We had set out on a four-to-five day trek from Long Layu, our starting point to Apauping, but like Gilligan's Island, our 3-hour tour had gone from a short jaunt to an 18-day trek and survival scenario.

Our realization that things had changed came slowly at first, but we soon had a growing awareness that our plans had gone astray. Mukhtar and I were not clear where we were, but we knew we were in the wrong place, on our own, and that our rendezvous with local guides had gone very wrong. We had minimal food, no maps of any decent scale (there are none for that area that I could find), no rifle, or shotgun. We would soon find out that our line-of-sight radio was of very limited value.

When we realized that things had gone wrong, we took stock of where we were. The 'trail' or path we had followed to our current location had been convoluted; even the local porters had stopped at times to verify we were heading in the right direction.

The weather for the last few days had been rainy and cloudy. Despite common perceptions of the jungle, there is some choice in the weather. You can choose between muggy and humid; overcast, rainy or cloudy. Sometimes the rain drizzles, sometimes it down-pours. There are typically 7 to 8 inches of rain per month in Long Layu; daytime temperatures average 79-81 degrees Fahrenheit and drop to an average of 64 degrees Fahrenheit at night.

We were at the bottom of a drainage with tall trees overhead and there was no clear path forward or back. The route we had tried to follow was one that was declining in importance due to shifting travel patterns across interior Borneo.

» *How do you sense that things are about to change in your life?*

    Steve Camkin

The situation Mukhtar and I found ourselves in definitely had the potential for even more dire headlines if we incurred an injury. 'Survival' shows on television have become more and more popular. We, however, had no camera crew hovering over our shoulders and no pre-scouted food sources. Mukhtar and I would have to survive in the rainy and non-fruit season.

There are degrees of being lost. Mukhtar and I knew the general area we were in. We knew the planned trail was a total of about 40 miles, although that does not fully account for the challenges of significant and frequent changes in elevation, slippery footing, and wading along winding streams and rivers. We knew some general directions we could head towards villages and we had some sense of what the landscape might be like. What we could not find was the original, specific path we had planned on traveling.

As we traveled, we became less 'lost'. The media later portrayed us as having been lost and then rescued. By the time Mukhtar and I met up with the military and villagers from Apauping, we knew what district we were in, what river we were on, where we were on the Bahau River and that we were about 18km from Apauping. We had done a lot of wandering because we could not find a clear and consistent trail, either forward or backward.

During moments of downtime in the jungle, one of the things I pondered was whether this experience was some form of payback or karma. During my time as an outdoors instructor, I had often taken corporate groups into an area we called 'The Maze' and asked them to find their way back. The area was a confusing jumble of house-sized rocks, arroyos, and meandering trails. We used it as a metaphor for exploring situations when groups are faced with uncertainty and difficulty in finding a way forward. I remember one corporate group in particular. The group was lost and yet was determined to find a way through the maze by pushing forward and climbing over the slabs and cliffs despite the risks. I stopped them to give them time to re-think. It was then that the only woman in the group was finally heard. She had been carefully paying attention to the landscape and was easily able to guide the group out safely. Mukhtar and I would now need to figure a way out of our situation or wait until help found us.

This four-to-five day jungle trek was supposed to be one section of a planned 60-day human-powered trek using only 'boots, bikes and paddles' to connect some of the trails, roads, and rivers through remnants of the once-vast jungles of interior Borneo.

Is life a journey or a jigsaw puzzle? Most expeditions can be described using the image of a journey. This expedition was more like a jigsaw puzzle with no corners and few straight edges. Instead of a straightforward linear journey, I was planning to do one piece of the larger expedition at a time; the sequence of the pieces being based on factors like weather, river levels, and availability of porters. Each piece of the overall expedition would need to be joined together at some point. It was an exercise in flexible scheduling and also adaptability.

If you have ever completed a large jigsaw puzzle, you know there is a significant risk of underestimating the number of steps in assembling the puzzle and the effort required to persevere beyond the easy steps. You may spend a lot of time organizing the pieces; you may need to undo some steps. It is tempting to leave things half-finished.

> » *Do you envision life as a linear journey?*

> » *Might there be some advantages to approaching life situations more like a jigsaw puzzle?*

We all find ourselves lost at some point in our lives and struggling to find our way. I am writing this book in 2020 amid the ever-changing landscape of the COVID-19 pandemic. Many of us are trying to navigate a new world into which we have been dropped into by circumstances related to COVID-19. In this book, Mukhtar and I relate our story of being left in the Borneo jungle, being lost, navigating our way through dense jungle and convoluted, overgrown paths, and managing our survival until we were able to make it to the small village we were hoping to reach. Our story wanders around as we did, sometimes looking forward, sometimes looking back.

> » *When have you felt lost or disoriented in your life?*
>
> » *What did that experience feel like?*

What does it mean to be 'lost'? Two of the most common questions Mukhtar and I were asked earlier in our expedition while trekking from Long Bawan to Long Layu, our starting point for the trek, were: *Mau Ke Mana*—Where are you going? and *Anda Berasal Dari Mana*—Where have you come from? That was usually followed by puzzled looks and comments of amazement at how far we were planning on traveling—and why we were traveling on foot when it was possible to travel by 4WD. Our answer was "for the challenge" (tatangan). The local people in Borneo were asking their questions literally, for example, what village are you traveling to? We could also ask the questions as a metaphor for life. The closest comparison to the western concept of challenge that I could find in Indonesian culture is the concept of pesalai. "The purpose of the pesalai is to acquire wealth and social status. In many ways, these are also spiritual journeys and provide an opportunity for young men and women to establish or enhance their sense of self" (Hansen 1989, p.148). Many people around the world are exploring these types of questions as a metaphor for their lives.

One of the challenges I have in sharing the story of Mukhtar and my trek has been around defining 'lost'. One common definition involves being unable to find ones way and not knowing one's whereabouts. Other words associated with 'lost' include astray, off-course, off-track, disoriented, having lost one's bearings, or going around in circles.

If your frame is "I am lost" (kalah), there is a strong chance you will feel disoriented and out of control. If your frame is "I am exploring a new way to get there", there can be a sense of adventure (petualangan), wonder (bertanya-tanya) and excitement (kegembiraan). Were Mukhtar and I lost? From one perspective, we were disoriented and off-track from our original course and timing; from another perspective, we were actively charting an alternative path to find our way. Many people, especially in the time of the COVID-19 pandemic and the challenges it brings, are expressing a sense of being lost; people are uncertain which way to go, or of being off-track from their original plans. I am also seeing people starting to find their way, often along a new path. For some, that path has been even more interesting, more of an adventure, than what they had planned. For others, both the old and new paths are a struggle along ill-defined trails that people have to clear as they push forward.

Jay Woodman writes

> life is a repeated cycle of getting lost and then finding yourself again. There are many smaller cycles within that cycle where you get lost to a smaller degree and then remember yourself again. Sometimes you do it to yourself on purpose, consciously, or unconsciously. Every time you get lost it is so that you can learn something or experience something from a different perspective. (Woodman, n.d.)

Yes, our wandering caused significant inconvenience to others. Yet wandering can also have benefits, in helping us find new goals to pursue, new ways to look at relationships, fresh views of our world, and new approaches to doing things. J.R.R. Tolkien wrote in The Lord of The Rings that "Not all those who wander are lost."

> » *How often do you know exactly where you are in your life?*
>
> » *Do you permit yourself to wander?*
>
> » *How can you wander in a way that minimizes the risk and negative consequences to you and others?*

As my Borneo trek continued, and after I returned home, I discovered that I was not the only one to feel lost at times in the vast green ocean that is the Borneo jungle. Hansen describes his experience:

> For the two weeks, we traversed a perilously rough area of thickly forested hills crisscrossed by countless unnamed waterways. During the time we were in this area I was completely lost. No sun, no distant view, and no clues on the map to give me even the illusion that I knew where we were. But what did it matter if I was lost? I was in a beautiful, untouched forest where there was plenty of game and I was content to relish the company of my two companions. (1988, pp. 132–133)

The Neuroscience of Being Lost. Research has shed some light on how people navigate.

> There is an elaborate system involving the hippocampus and other areas of the brain for creating an analog of the world and your motion, position, and direction of travel within it. …Place cells and other cells involved in navigation are constantly being reprogrammed [remapped] … Interestingly, the Hippocampus, which tells you where you are and where you're going (if the map is right), does not control the seeking of a goal. The urge to get to a specific place, the drive toward a goal, appears to be emotional… The brain is reaching out through the senses, bringing

information in, attempting to grasp the environment, and wire up a map. The input and output of the hippocampus and other areas are being sent to the amygdala to establish a drive toward beneficial things and an aversion to harmful things. (Gonzales, 2004, p.157)

The amygdala is wired to respond with action (fight or flight) not reason.

Admitting that you are lost is difficult because having no mental map, being no place, is like having no self: It's impossible to conceive because one of the main jobs of the organism is to adjust itself to place. (Gonzales, 2004, p.159)

'Woods shock' describes a state of loss of spatial orientation that can lead to inexplicable actions like abandoning full backpacks or neglecting efforts to make fire or shelter. (Gonzales, 2004, p.165)

In daily life, people operate on the necessary illusion that they know where they are. Most of the time, they don't. The only time most people are not lost to some degree is when they are home. It's quite possible to know the route from one place to another without knowing precisely where you are. …Nevertheless, most people normally have enough route knowledge to get them where they are going. If they don't…they get lost. It's simple. All you have to do is to fail to update your mental map then persist in following it even when the landscape…tries to tell you you are wrong. (Gonzales, 2004, p. 163)

"Being lost then is not a location; it is a transformation. It can happen in the woods or it can happen in life" (Gonzales, 2004, p. 166).

Steve Camkin

» *When do you feel lost?*

» *What transformations are you, or those around you facing?*

Another definition of 'lost' is "something that has been taken away or cannot be recovered" (Lost, 2020). I struggle with this deficit-based view. I felt like I had gained from the unplanned experience Mukhtar and I had in the Borneo jungle. I got to know Mukhtar at a deep level, I experienced the incredible compassion, concern, and inclusiveness of the people of Apauping and Long Layu, and I received an opportunity to stretch my limits. I also saw wildlife and sights I would not have otherwise seen.

There have been, of course, other planned expeditions in Borneo that turned into near-survival situations. Mueller's Borneo crossing expedition in 1824 was nearly successful but ended in tragedy. As 'a consolation', he has a Gibbon and a mountain range named after him. A major expedition by Dr. A.W. Nieuwenhuis had "...crossed the island in 1897 with 110 porters, two associates, and bodyguards but it had taken them a year" (Hansen, 1988, p.45). Stories of more successful expeditions include Hansen's (1988) first known crossing Borneo, East to West by a White person, and O'Hanlon's (1987) journey in 1984 in Sarawak and Northern Kalimantan. The successful expeditions used more of a lightweight style relying on just a few local guides, using local resources, and a limited amount of imported equipment.

There are other memorable stories of people being subjected to trials in the jungle. Ghinsberg's (2006) ordeal of being lost on his own for three weeks in the Amazonian jungle has been made into a movie. Ken Wilson struggled out of the Mexican jungle after 20 days, losing 50 pounds and gathering an impressive collection of mosquito and crab bites (Corrigan & Fitzmaurice, 2012).

Seventeen-year-old Juliann Koepcke fell 10,000' into the Amazonian rainforest when the plane in which she was flying broke apart in mid-air after encountering a severe thunderstorm. She survived the fall, 11 days alone in the Peruvian jungle, and navigated her way alone downstream until she was eventually found (Koepcke, 2012). The situation Mukhtar and I found ourselves in was certainly not as serious, or sustained, like that of some other survival stories, however, I believe there are life and leadership lessons to be learned from our story as well as the stories of Ghinsberg, Wilson, Koepcke, and others.

Life's challenges can be 'crucibles' for personal and leadership development. Consultants Bennis and Thomas concluded that

> ...one of the most reliable indicators and predictors of true leadership is an individual's ability to find meaning in negative events and to learn from even the most trying circumstances... the skills required to conquer adversity and emerge stronger and more committed than ever are the same ones that make for extraordinary leaders. [They] came to call the experiences that shape leaders 'crucibles', after the vessels medieval alchemists used in their attempts to turn base metals into gold. For the leaders we interviewed, the crucible experience was a trial and a test, a point of deep self-reflection that forced them to question who they were and what mattered to them. It required them to examine their values, question their assumptions, hone their judgment. And, invariably, they emerged from the crucible stronger and more sure of themselves and their purpose—changed in some fundamental way. Leadership crucibles can take many forms. Some are violent, life-threatening events. Others are more prosaic episodes of self-doubt. But whatever the crucible's nature, the people we spoke with were able...to create a narrative around it, a story of how they were challenged, met the challenge and became better leaders. (Bennis & Thomas, 2002)

Sports Psychologists have a term they use to describe some athlete's responses to adversity-adversarial growth. "The struggle against an obstacle inevitably propels the fighter to a new level of functioning. The extent of the struggle determines the extent of growth. The obstacle is the advantage, not the adversary" (Holiday, 2014, p.57). When you are yourself developing or helping others through a challenge, it is important to remember the concept of Optimum Stress or Optimum Arousal. "Each of us has a different stress threshold—that is, the degree of stress needed to benefit or harm us—depending on our history and even our genetic makeup" (Singer, 2012). Enough stress helps motivate us towards our goals; too much stress adversely impacts performance. One way to test your own or others' level of Optimum Stress is to take on increasing levels of challenge in a task and observe the impacts on your learning and performance.

> » *What have been your crucible' experiences?*

> » *Did you just suffer through them or did you find some meaning and learning in them?*

As well as my interest in 'crucible' experiences I have long been fascinated by why, in survival situations, some people give up easily and die while others, sometimes more poorly equipped, find resilience, a reason to persevere, and a means to survive. Survivor research looking at resilience and the will to live has taken popular (Siebert, 2001), psychological (Bennet, 1983), and autobiographical (Richards & McEwan, 1989) approaches.

John Leach (2011) is a survival researcher exploring cognitive factors such as loss of executive functioning and short-term memory amongst people who have been in survival situations. Leach asks a very different question than the usual one of "why did this person survive?". Leach (2011) says

we should ask why so many people die when there is no need. In other words, it is not the 'will-to-live', but the 'want-to-live' that matters.

Consider this example. In 1994 a light aircraft crashed in the Sierra Nevada. Of the three people on board, one passenger was trapped in the wreckage, another had no more than superficial bruising, whilst the pilot had apparent injuries to his arm, ankle, and ribs. To obtain help the pilot walked for 11 days through the snow-covered mountains before reaching a road and flagging down a passing car. The alerted rescue services located the crash site. Both the pilot's companions were dead (NTSB, 1995).

Media attention was given to the feat of the endurance of the injured pilot in traveling for 11 days over snow-covered mountains to seek help. His two dead companions warranted no more than a passing sentence in the press. Yet, one of these men had no more than superficial bruising following the crash. So why did he die? The material was there for shelter; fire could be made; water was available, and he would not have starved in 11 days. This is the crux of survival psychology. (Leach, 2011, p. 26)

Leach (2011) notes that "...when life is threatened cognitive functioning is impaired (p.26)." This impairment can show up in several ways. Executive functioning is a collection of mental skills including flexible thinking, self-control and working memory that assists with two primary tasks: "Organization: Gathering information and structuring it for evaluation [and] regulation: Taking stock of your surroundings and changing behavior in response to it. Impaired Executive Functioning often manifests in crises as 'brain lock,' or a lack of initiative" (Bhandari, 2019).

The brain also operates with 'normalcy bias'. When thrown into a crisis some people may suffer from a credulity response where they just don't believe what is happening. This "denial and inactivity prepares people well for the victim role" (Holiday, 2014).

» *What might Leach's research tell us about individual reactions in survival situations, about employee disengagement, or about who "gives up" in the face of challenging circumstances in business?*

Sometimes in this book, you will see my diary notes written in the moment. My diary notes are indicated by italicized text. Usually, these notes were made at the end of the day while I was huddling under the plastic tarp that was our shelter. In places, I have added comments to my diary notes for clarification. These comments are indicated by regular text. Reflection questions are included at various points in the story and are indicated by indentation and italicized text.

Sometimes my diary notes are out of sequence; sometimes I am not even sure if I have the actual days recorded correctly. On the days where the notes are sparse, please ascribe that to my lack of discipline, or to the strong focus on survival and on managing our energy. Time was ambiguous and distorted during the days we were in the jungle. Mukhtar and I measured time more in estimated days to get to our intended destination, rather than by a calendar. My diary notes got further scrambled when I took the wire out of my notebook to fashion a rough fishhook. Writing now, sheltering in place during the time of COVID-19, I am experiencing some of the same disorientation. I just put the garbage cans out in the street four days ahead of pickup; I find myself constantly checking my calendar to confirm what day it is. It is again hard to keep track of the days and dates.

The jungle is an environment that tests a person's resilience-physically, mentally, and emotionally. There are multiple simultaneous stressors, progress is usually slow, and visibility is normally restricted. My purpose in telling the story of Mukhtar and I in the Borneo jungle is not just to remember the experience, but also to learn (or relearn) and share some lessons that can be more broadly applied to life and leadership. We all have stories of resilience, challenges overcome, or at least faced down. There are many books on resilience and adaptability and the topics are especially current today. This book is our story, our collection of lessons learned on this 'adventure', and some thoughts on how to apply those lessons more broadly to life. Our goal in writing is to explore and uncover our sources of resilience for challenges that we all may encounter-personal challenges, challenges in our families, challenges in our organizations and communities.

Mukhtar and I will share some of the strategies that helped us survive, and adapt to, the situation in which we unexpectedly found ourselves. We will also share some of the skills the Dyak and Penan people have used over centuries to thrive in the dynamic environment that is the Borneo jungle. I will share some of the concepts and tools related to personal and organizational resilience that I have used in coaching, training, and consulting work with organizations around the globe. These ideas and concepts also served Mukhar and me well during our jungle experience. Most important is the notion that we can not only survive challenges by adapting but that we can emerge stronger from whatever jungle we are finding our way through. We hope you will find some value in our story and use it to find your inner resilience.

2

WHERE ARE WE?
HOW DID WE GET HERE?

*"Travel is the act of leaving familiarity behind.
Destination is merely a by-product of the journey."*
ERIC HANSEN

Imagine you are rafting down a river and have just been dumped out of your raft at the top of a Class IV or V rapid. You may have been suddenly forced underwater, thrown around, and feel like the air has been knocked out of you. You may have noticed your instinctive attempt to breathe before surfacing. That will only worsen the situation. The correct action is actually counter-intuitive. You should breathe *out* in tiny bubbles to avoid taking in water. During disorientation, some people panic or take actions that make things worse for themselves or others. In the turbulence, we often ask questions like: Where am I? Which way is up? What happened? How did I get here?

A common experience in survival or crisis situations, whether a rafting incident, an unexpected divorce, a sudden job loss, losing someone dear to you, or the kind of situation Mukhtar and I found ourselves in, is disorientation. So, before we dive into some of the lessons learned let's pause, get oriented, paint a picture of where Mukhtar and I were, and how we got there.

Our story took place in Borneo, the third-largest island in the world, and a place of some mystique even today despite more than 30% of its massive tropical forests having been logged in the last few decades (Nuwer, 2014). The island has a long human history. Cave paintings of wild cattle dated to between 40,000-52,000 years ago were discovered in Jeriji Saleh cave in East Kalimantan (Plutniak, S. *et al*, 2014).

I have been fascinated with the area ever since reading stories in high school about the nomadic Penan tribe and the head-hunting Dyak. My interest was further fueled in later years while poring over maps in various state and university libraries and when reading books such as *Into the Heart of Borneo* (O'Hanlon, 1987) and *A Journey Among the Peoples of Central Borneo in Word and Picture* (Tillema, 1989), the story of a 1938 expedition. Like many visitors to Borneo, I was attracted by romantic historical notions of the jungle and by its people and their culture. Over multiple trips to Borneo, I have grown to admire many aspects of the lifestyle of the local people and the way they have first adapted to the jungle, and later to the challenges posed by a rapidly changing environment.

Within their environment, the Penan are masters of adaptation. Hanbury-Tennison records an early experience with nomadic Penan a number of decades ago:

> ... their life cycle appears deceptively simple: they pursue the herds of wild boar and gather the wild sago...It is, in reality much more complicated than that. For a start, no group will encroach on the territory of another, and the routes of their annual migrations will be affected by many factors, including where the boar go and when the sago and wild fruits ripen. (p.66)

Because they move so often, usually at intervals of between ten days and three weeks, nomadic Penan houses are very simple and can be erected very quickly. Usually, they are built high up on ridges where there are fewer mosquitoes and sandflies and where they are safer from falling trees. This may mean that water has to be fetched in bamboo tubes from a stream far below, but the Penan drink very little, getting most of their liquid from their food, especially sago. (p.69)

Penan culture has some unique aspects. "Everything is always scrupulously divided among the group, however little may have been hunted or gathered...There is no Penan word for 'thank you.' It is simply assumed that everything will be shared" (Hanbury-Tennison, 2017, p.67).

Like any other culture, Penan culture has adapted and evolved in response to environmental challenges and opportunities. Regarding food for example,

every morsel of the animal is eaten, the offal, eyes, brain and bone marrow being recognized as the most nutritious parts which are usually given to the children. These parts also provide the minerals and salt they need and make up for the fact that they eat few if any green vegetables, although they do harvest lots of different fruits in their season. (Hanbury-Tennison, 2017, p.67)

Large ants (ketungan) are sometimes added to cooking food as a substitute for salt (Puri, 2005, p.153).

Blowpipes were previously made from bamboo before the Penan were able to trade for iron or smelt the iron themselves. Sometimes the Penan will use their blowpipe to suck up water from a stream. Hardwood versions of blowguns are more accurate but require "...laborious drilling with a long metal bar through a solid piece [of hardwood timber]." (Hanbury-Tennison, p.68)

Because of the depletion of the forests in Kalimantan, the present indigenous hunters need a hunting weapon that can be shot over a much greater distance than the blowgun. Therefore, some Basap people living [in] Kalimantan Timur, have constructed sophisticated air guns powered by strings of elastic, which shoot these poison darts accurately at a distance of about 100 meters. (Zahorka 2004a:10)

Today rifles or shotguns are the weapons that are most used in the jungle for hunting.

Poison for blowgun darts was extracted from the latex of the *Antiaris Toxicaria* tree, a process that requires some clever processing. To dehydrate the milky latex into a paste, a long, carefully implemented procedure is essential because the steroid glycoside compound is extremely heat-sensitive.

Therefore, hunters perform the dehydration of the latex by using a young leaf from the small Licuala spinosa palm. The leaf is folded into a boat-shaped container to hold the latex at a carefully determined distance over a small flame for about one week. This is possible because the young Licuala leaf is astonishingly fireproof and durable. This is the secret of producing the lethal poison. If the latex were heated at too high a temperature, the glycoside compound would crack and its toxicity would be lost. (Zahorka, 2006)

The Penan are a settled people now, but still display amazing jungle skills and adaptability to their environment. I spent some time with settled Penan near Long Kerong a few years ago, traveling there by light plane, 4WD, long-tail boat, and on foot.

Dyak tribes were renowned for head-hunting. The days of head-hunting are now long gone, however, recollections and remnants of this past culture still exist. On previous treks to Bario in the Central Highlands and Tanjung Lokang in West Kalimantan, I had seen parangs (the local version of a machete) inlaid with small gold dots. Each dot represented a head that had been taken. The parangs had once been owned by the grandfathers of the present owners. In Sarawak, Malaysia I had visited longhouses where heads were still on display in the rafters of meeting houses and blow-guns were mounted on the walls. On this most recent expedition, Mukhtar and I would climb up a 45-foot log and vine ladder at a place called Catch-Kill, a frequent ambush site over several hundred years for tribes traveling through a narrow pass.

Views of the human and nature interaction in the Borneo jungle have shifted over the years. Hansen writes that interior communities of Borneo "...used to live in what anthropologists call 'primitive affluence.' With few exceptions, everything the people needed came from the jungle. There was an abundance of fish and wild game and building materials; medicine and plant foods were easily obtainable" (1988, pp. 42-43). In reality, trading across jungle trails, and up and down rivers, has occurred for centuries. Today agriculture,

Steve Camkin

timber harvesting, coal, palm oil, and other resource development projects have drastically altered the economies of interior villages.

On this expedition I was hoping to see some of the once great forests and experience something of the indigenous cultures before they were changed forever. I had heard, for example, that a lot of the jungle trails between villages were falling into disuse or had been replaced by roads. Like Hansen, I thought that perhaps less change had occurred deep in the interior. What I would come to understand more clearly was that

> In both ecology and ecological anthropology, the extreme notions of pristine, undisturbed nature, and humans living in harmonious relationship with their environment have given way to a less absolute and more pragmatic view of the environment that is dynamic and subject to non-equilibrium processes. (Puri, 2005, p.7)

Highly venomous sea snakes, as well as sharks, live in the offshore waters. Large Salt-water Crocodiles cruise the mangroves closer in. On an earlier expedition, I had mistakenly paddled up to what I thought was a log drifting offshore. The water exploded as the 'log' thrashed wildly past my boat and then submerged. The croc was longer than my 12-foot folding sea kayak. Later on that same trip while celebrating the completion of my five-day open ocean kayak trip, I had jumped off the dock and landed 8 feet away from several deadly, but almost invisible Box Jellyfish (*Chironex Flekeri*).

Those hazards are in the ocean. Other risks await in the jungle. On a previous trip across Borneo from East to West, I learned that my guide's Grandmother had died from a scorpion sting. Mukhtar also told me of a close encounter he had with a cobra in one of the areas we would later trek through in our expedition. I brought tablets with me for Malaria although the area we would be in was mostly free of the disease. Other fatalities in the past had occurred in encounters with Pygmy Elephants (ANZAC, n.d.). Most of those

Pygmy Elephants are gone now. There are still the more mundane, but very real risks of trips, slips, and falls on tricky terrain, or drowning on river crossings in remote areas.

Apart from life-threatening hazards, there are numerous other mere discomforts or irritations: constant rain, smothering humidity, spiked vines of all descriptions, mosquitoes, sand flies, fire ants, and leeches. On a previous trip across Borneo, I had counted over 300 leeches on me in one day before I gave up counting by mid-afternoon. The leeches had marched in waves across vines and leaves at head height, across mossy rocks on the edge of the river when I stopped to rest, and seemingly just dropped from the sky as I walked past. Anchored at one end, they waved in the air for a sign of their next victim.

The Thread Leech is named for its ability to stretch out like a thread extending its reach. It prefers to attack the mouth and nose so the Dusan people when drinking from a stream "…assemble a spout which they fashion from leaves or bamboo" (O'Hanlon, 1987, p.88).

A Fire Ant's ferocious bite "allows them to get a grip, but what really hurts is what comes next, the sting from their abdomen. It also happens to be where they get their name from, as the sensation is likened to the feeling of fire" (Borneo Nature Foundation, 2013).

Heat is one of the first ways disorientation hits trekkers in Borneo. The heat whacks you on the side of the head like a tackle from a 225-pound rugby player and grinds you into the ground, finally letting you up after a few days of acclimatization. Pelton comments: "the heat slams you down like a drunk in a bar fight. It is so hot the color is shattered into shimmering waves that make you blink" (2007, p. 11). Some good advice from someone who had been to Borneo before: "Acclimatize slowly. …You'll think it is the end of the world. You can't breathe. And then after two weeks you'll be used to it. And once in the jungle proper you will never want to come out" (O'Hanlon, 1987, p.6).

The area in which Mukhtar and I became lost on this expedition was part of Indonesian Borneo in Central Kalimantan province, close to the Malaysian border.

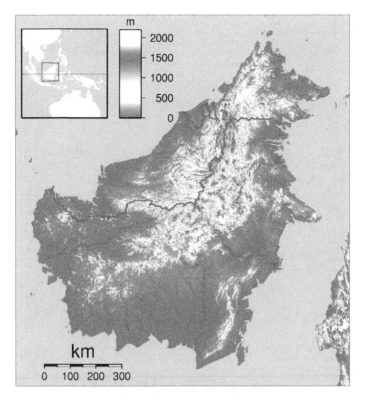

On the map it is in the northern section a little south and east of the roughly 90 degree bend that indicates the boundary between Malaysia and Indonesia.

*https://commons.wikimedia.org/wiki/File:Borneo_
    Locator_Topography.png*
*https://upload.wikimedia.org/wikipedia/commons/b/
    be/Borneo_Locator_Topography.png*

Below is a photo of a tourist map that shows the villages of Long Layu (top left corner) and Apauping (labeled on this map as Apan Ping). Apauping is located upriver of Long Alango towards the center and bottom of the map. The map includes roads that have not yet been constructed and some that have fallen into disuse.

DECEMBER 10TH, 2019
Tarakan

My first impression of Mukhtar was noted in my journal: "*Mukhtar is from Sulawesi and he started guiding in 1984. He has guided in many places in Borneo, in Papua, including a 2-week trip to reach un-contacted tribes, and in Sulawesi. Mukhtar is shorter than I expected but looks very strong. He speaks good English-which will make things a lot easier for me. He seems pleased to get a long trek and a 45-day 'gig'.*"

Mukhtar has an easy laugh, and I quickly got the impression that he wanted us both to have a great time. I felt comfortable with him very quickly. I later learned from Mukhtar that I had initially come across to him as being 'serious.' He was concerned that I would blame him if anything went wrong. I think he got that impression while hearing me talking on my mobile phone while trying to work out some phone and banking issues with companies back in the US.

Steve Camkin

Mukhtar would help me plan how to travel from region to region; we would hire local guides and porters for those times when we needed additional local knowledge. Without Mukhtar's depth of experience, the trip would have been impossible. Apart from his technical skills, Mukhtar had mastered the art of asking questions indirectly and gently leading folks into a conversation. This was an essential skill in building goodwill with the local people whose land we would traverse, buy food from, and amongst whom we would hire porters and local guides.

Sometimes it takes a while to get to the starting line. To get to our starting point for this section of the trek, I had first flown on December 10th to Tarakan, close to the border with Sabah, a Malaysian state, and spent the night. From there my journal records that Mukhtar and I did some shopping for supplies and then on December 11th took "… *a 1.5 hour ride in what I call a coffin boat-it had only one exit, was totally enclosed, and very tightly packed with people. [From there] "we head across the open sea and then up several estuaries lined with Nipa Palms and passing klotoks [a traditional river boat], coal barges, and speed-boats to reach Tanjung Selor.*

From Tanjung Selor we flew the next day (December 12th) to Long Bawan in the interior. I like Pelton's description of the area as he flew over it: "We had flown over miles and miles of green undulating jungle of Borneo, a thick, mist-streaked carpet broken only by brown mud-swollen rivers that snaked like Chinese dragons (Pelton, 2007 p.45). That afternoon Mukhtar and I rented a 4WD and driver to take us to the border with the Malaysian state of Sarawak.

The 4WD driver dropped us off and we slogged back to Long Bawan through what seemed like rivers of deep red mud that foreshadowed even more of the same for the next day.

My shoes were caked with many pounds of red mud, as were my socks. Overnight, we prepared for an expected 8-hour hike to Long Layu, a Lun Dayeh village in the highlands of about 300 people, known for its 9 salt springs (Langub, 2012) and Adan rice grown using wet-rice farming techniques.

Adan rice (white, black, or red) is known for its small grain, fine texture, and pleasant taste (Hului, 2019a). There is a legend that tells of how the salt springs were discovered.

Long time ago, the whole area of *Krayan* Highlands was a thick forest. Then came a man who saw that there were many pigeons (burung punai) in the area. So the man took out his blowpipe and shot one of the birds. He quickly dressed the bird, plucking out its feathers. As he was looking for a water source to clean the bird, the man saw there was a spring nearby. After washing the bird, he returned home, where he quickly roasted it. Once the man tasted the bird, he was overwhelmed by its taste. He wondered what could have made the bird taste so delicious. So the man returned to where he caught the bird, retracing his steps until he figured out that it must have been the water which made the bird tasty. He dipped his finger into the spring and discovered that the water was actually salty. The man then told his fellow villagers about his find, and they started to cook their dishes using the saltwater from the spring. At first, they just poured the saltwater into their dishes when they cooked. Eventually, the villagers figured out how to process the saltwater into brine, and it has been practiced by the residents of Krayan Highlands for generations. (Hului, 2019b)

Salt and rice may seem like simple things, yet the introduction of salt has impacted styles of cooking, culture, social-economic activities and relationships with their surroundings and beyond (Langub, 2012). The road that now connects Long Layu with Malaysia has enabled increased exports of rice and brought rising affluence in Long Layu.

DECEMBER 13TH, 2019
Long Bawan to Long Layu

The adventure began in earnest the next morning, a push along a relatively new road through jungle, farmland, and a few villages. *Left at 7:30 after breakfast. 12 hours of mud-slog. The last two hours in the dark. Road chopped up by wheel ruts. One bogged vehicle. One broken bridge. 80-100m sections of mud pools. Some greasy-gray mud but mostly orange clay. Mud extends right across the road. Where there is no mud there are stony sections.*

Tried using Adidas Kampong shoes but very hard on the feet on stony sections. Adidas Kampong, cheap soccer-style plastic shoes, gave better traction on the jungle floor than western-style boots. *Two small blisters but caught them in time and did some quick first aid on them.*

During preliminary planning, *I had estimated this as one or possibly two days in our program. Before we started out and became familiar with the conditions Mukhtar expected 7-8 hours.* We decided to try to do it in one day but had some equipment with us in case we needed to over-night along the way. *Glad we sent most of our equipment ahead or it would have been 16 hours+ with all the extra weight, slipping and sliding. ...Road was built four years ago.* Roads in Borneo are constantly being rebuilt.

I remember someone in Bario, a Kelabit Highlands town, saying five years before that there was a track between Lembudud and Long Layu. *Until the road went in villagers walked the narrow trail. They took a buffalo travois to shop for groceries. The price for a buffalo before the road was built was 25 million Indonesian Rupiah IR or $1,720 U.S.D.; after the road 6.5 Million IR or $446 U.S.D.. We passed lots of jungle and passed rice paddies*

near kampongs. With the road now cut, lots of local villagers are cutting trees for their own construction purposes. I have mixed feelings about this. I want people to have the conveniences of modern life, but I am concerned that unchecked usage will mean that the forest resources will not be there for future generations. *Passed buffaloes grazing at the road edge, tethered by a rope through a nose ring.*

Some white egrets (kuntul putih) hanging out with the buffalo (kerbau). Saw two hornbills (ranking) fly over the mountaintops and watched them for a while.

Flying downhill in the twilight then in the dark on mud-tracks at hour 11. I was having a "flow" moment- feeling very fast, but in control. I was bouncing between 15-inch ruts on the road within two-foot drops on either side. Ankle busting territory on reflection, but it felt like I was back in my best trail-running days. Jackson (2011) describes flow as an altered state of consciousness wherein performance level, satisfaction, and happiness all rise. You become one with whatever you are doing, you feel utterly absorbed and enjoy intrinsic rewards as you do the activity. Your skills sharpen to meet the demands of the challenges, and everything falls into place. …it is like tapping into your best self, where who you are and what you are doing fall into perfect alignment and harmony. (pp. 12-13)

» *What moments of "flow" have you had in your life?*

» *What might these moments tell you about your best self and the strengths you can bring to bear when you need to find resilience?*

What I did not know at the time was that Mukhtar was concerned about me running into a snake that might be soaking up the last heat reflected off the road. Borneo has 160 species of snakes including the King Cobra which grows to 18 feet, the Equatorial Spitting Cobra, and the Reticulated Python. Specimens of the latter have been found up to 30 feet in length. O'Hanlon notes, comfortingly, that there are "…really only 6 species of very dangerous snakes in Borneo: two cobras, two kraits and two coral snakes" (1987, p.112). One snake I was hoping to see was a Twin-Barred Tree Snake, a spectacular flying snake. "They can draw in the belly so that the underside becomes hollow and the snake is shaped like a split bamboo, and then by launching themselves from a branch they can make a controlled glide" (O'Hanlon, 1987, p.112).

After dark, we walked into a homestay, ate some simple food, and took a bucket bath to wash the mud off. Some news of the outside world comes via text from my dear friend…Australia is suffering from massive bushfires, 15 tourists have died in a volcanic eruption in New Zealand, and US politics is in turmoil.

DECEMBER 14TH, 2019
Long Layu

Up at about 7:30 to organize porters, wash clothes and check gear. Drama this morning. Mukhtar is having problems finding porters who know the way to Apauping. There is one old man with a heart condition, one man working on a construction project and one other whose location is currently unknown. Waiting game. M has done part of the next section but 5 years ago.

Especially since the introduction of the road, fewer people are making the trek from Long Layu to Apauping. Local knowledge of trails was rapidly being lost. Hansen, in his cross-Borneo travels in the late 1980s, reported the same issue after the introduction of flights into the interior: "The jungle paths to the highlands had disappeared years before because few people used them... What had traditionally been a two or three-week journey on foot through the jungle can now be done in forty-five minutes by air" (Hansen, 2000, p.59). Roads are now opening up the interior. It is now cheaper and easier to travel back to Long Bawan and across the border to Malaysia by 4WD than to hike to the small village of Apauping on the Upper Bahau River. Until the introduction of air travel and the rapid intrusion of roads in the 1960s, most travel in Borneo had been along the river systems and on foot-trails cutting across mountain passes. Part of the motivation for my trip had been to learn how the culture was changing as a result of shifts in transportation.

We judged it prudent to find locals with more recent and more complete knowledge of the route. I have used the term "trails" previously, but in reality, except close to major settlements, routes would be a more accurate term-a general direction with key landscape markers along the way. Trail maintenance is only done by those using the trail, not by paid workers, and is not regularly scheduled. Since cutting or re-cutting trails is hard work, the focus is just on clearing enough of the vegetation to get through for the moment.

Mukhtar and I anticipated having problems finding people and the route in this area; those challenges were larger than we expected. Limited communications, changing weather, changing schedules based on weather and emerging projects, and declining usage and knowledge of the local jungle trails were all factors that meant we had to do most of our planning after arrival in Long Layu rather than in advance.

We plan to prioritize contacting the "unknown location" person first (Plan A). Plan B is to pay the boss of the paddy worker extra money to release him while also paying the porter a salary. We are also offering a finder's fee to anyone finding suitable porters with local knowledge of the trail. It sounds like this trail has fallen into disuse somewhat. The way to keep the trail alive is to walk it.

> » *What knowledge are you losing by not 'walking the trail' (regularly using what you know)?*

Plan C might be more 'road-bashing' around the Apokayan region but that would be disappointing. I had heard stories of the deep, untracked forest there that sounded intriguing. *I've been poring over regional maps looking at re-routing options. We were ahead two days and I have spare days built into the end of my itinerary we can use if necessary.*

While waiting for return phone calls M tells me some stories of a client fainting after hours of walking in the dark and holding the back of his t-shirt after the client insisted on pushing on. Also of getting lost on the East-West crossing route for days many years ago, and also of being helped out by logging workers and coming across a Penan native many years ago still wearing a bark loin cloth. Mukhtar has certainly had some real exploratory adventures. Tom Harrison wrote, "The Punans have a quality of stillness…They melt into the shadows and that is their life" (1938, p.9).

Hansen who spent six years trading and traveling across interior Borneo noted that

> the Penan are regarded by all the inland villagers as *ahli hutan*, the forest experts. …To the Penan the jungle is a self-maintaining garden/warehouse from which they collect food as well as certain saleable items such as damar (tree resin), beozar stones, edible swiftlet nests, and gaharu. (Hanson, 2000, p.137)

> This dark, scented [Gaharu] wood is only found as an abnormal growth on *Aquilaria* trees when it is infected with a type of mould, probably following an injury or insect attack. Used as an incense and as a medicine, it is one of the most expensive natural products in the world and can fetch as much as $100,000 a kilogram today. Just think how rich the Penan could be if they could still find it in their depleted forests, but it is rare now-because the *Aquilaria* trees, although protected, have mostly been felled by loggers. (Hanbury-Tennison, p.72)

The Penan have a deep knowledge of the resources available to them and regularly "…use at least 30 different plants as medicines for dressing wounds, treating rashes, curing stomachaches and headaches, counteracting poison and reducing fever" (Hanbury-Tennison, 2014, p. 68).

The deep knowledge of the jungle the Penan have not only helped them to live off the land but also to avoid other tribes. They were not head-hunters, although the tribes around them were. Some of the Penan retain jungle knowledge, but most have moved to larger towns where many are struggling to adapt to an urban lifestyle. Loss of traditional lands to logging, palm oil plantations and dams has been, and remains, a controversial issue in both Kalimantan, Indonesia and in the Malaysian states of Sarawak and Sabah. Some efforts are being made to preserve the cultural knowledge through eco-tourism efforts (Adventure Alternative, n.d.).

I tried to hand-wash my clothes in a basin but they come out orange after I put my socks in as well. 12:30 pm still no success finding porters. M seems to be getting a little stressed by that. M has a conversation with the home-stay owner about other possible routes to take if we cannot get porters; he is now on the phone again looking for porters. The latest call is more upbeat. There is a possibility to get porters from Long Layu to take us half-way and then have us meet porters from Apauping. We might need to wait in the jungle until the Apauping porters reach us.

I keep exploring other potential routes. One route to Apauping goes through Kabuan and a road is shown on the map, but local knowledge says this road does not exist. [Kabuan is another abandoned village site.] Another option is to take a 4WD to Poping (the next village) to seek out people with local knowledge there. We also talked about taking a boat to another village but we cannot find any gasoline. The road is apparently tough going at the moment and it would be difficult to get there.

Later in the day... *It sounds like we have porters confirmed now from the Apauping side-we just need to find porters from Long Layu. There are fewer porters around now as the road to the Malaysian border has made trips to Apauping, and downstream less necessary. We are expecting a 5-day trip. A bat (kelelawar) just flew through the dining room. I spent an hour walking around Long Layu taking pictures. Electricity is available from 6am-noon. Internet is very fussy.* There has been a big push for connectivity, but some towns in the highlands only recieved internet in the last 8-10 years. *Lots of chickens, lazy dogs, buffalo in yards. Kids are joking it up in front of me to get their picture taken. Lots of colorfully painted houses. A large buffalo stands his ground on the soccer field defending the goal post. I checked out the wreckage of a plane that had crashed on the old airstrip.*

Mukhtar is talking with someone outside the house now that

Steve Camkin

I think may be a potential porter for us. He looks like an aging, long-haired rock star. Just learned that the old guy used to porter but not anymore. *He used to search for Gaharu wood close to the Malaysia border. So much for my initial impressions; the guy had been hard-core in his younger days. Gaharu wood is used for making very expensive perfume.* One chunk that was found was worth 1.3 billion IR ($87,682). *His trips used to take him several months, often traveling at night, usually with just one other person.* Our short trip would be like a stroll in the local park to him. The perception of risk is partly what we are used to.

Just met the two younger porters who might travel with us. *One raced in the Heart of Borneo Challenge,* a grass-roots eco-tourism, multi-day race that celebrates stewardship of nature, culture, history, and fitness. *Lots of cross-checking on the meeting point where we will be dropped off and meet the Apauping porters. Loud frogs make it hard to go to sleep* [the Borneo equivalent of noisy neighbors]. One species recently discovered living in leaf litter in an adjacent region is called the Borneo Big Sticky Frog, named because when it is attacked it secretes poisonous mucus (Joomla, 2020).

DECEMBER 15TH, 2019
Long Layu

Roosters wake me up at 5am. Overcast, a little cool, and then raining in the morning. Sunny afternoon. Still waiting on a decision-will local porters go? Long Layu has lots of concrete trash bins but the pickup service has not started yet. Some houses have lots of trash underneath and also in drainages. Small ponds next to the houses contain small fish for food. The home-stay family has a dwarf boa in a cage by the fireplace that they feed rats and frogs.

Still waiting... one person is trying to locate a friend who has local knowledge but he cannot find him at the moment.

Met one potential porter who couldn't travel with us because of an injured foot. Mukhtar is acting as the equivalent of a hotel concierge. We have finally found two porters that are going to guide us about half-way to Apauping. We will meet other porters from Apauping at that point who will guide us to their village.

I walked around town again. Looked at a crashed aircraft alongside the airstrip. The landing strip is still usable but there are no scheduled flights now. Interior Borneo was partly opened up by planes flying into small grass landing strips like this. Prior to that, trips to many villages might take weeks using long-tail boats.

The Britten-Norman Islander was flown to Long Layu airstrip following an aircraft accident there four days earlier involving an Airvan. On takeoff it veered off the airstrip, into a muddy pond. The 1804-foot airstrip surface is grass and clay and become quite waterlogged after a downpour. The aircraft was withdrawn from use and the engines removed and most of the interior stripped. The aircraft was left at Long Layu (Aviation Safety Network, 2006).

» *How can you prevent errors on takeoff for your new projects?*

I watched the Nile Perch in the house pond eating spinach leaves. The snake is awake and moving around. I sat around the small fire (api). A black pig (babi) escaped from its cage and went running past the homestay with little kids, adults, and grandparents racing after it. One of the locals *came to the homestay to show us some pictures of his traditional dance group that was featured on TV. They were filmed at Batu Ning, a tall rock 1 to 2 days trek from Long Layu. Plans are now confirmed for a departure tomorrow. We will start by paddling in the morning. Game on!*

3

INTO THE UNKNOWN

*"I hope you never fear those mountains in the distance.
Never settle for the path of least resistance."*

LEE ANN WOMACK

DECEMBER 16TH, 2019
Long Layu to bush camp on the Sungai Bulu (Pa Ameb area)

False starts. *Today was a bit of a mess. After breakfast we made several stops around the village before finally heading down to the boats at about 10:15 or 10:30.*

I was surprised to see there were two boats and only two paddles, as the plan from yesterday was to have four paddles so we could paddle the first section upstream. Mukhtar was in one boat; I was in the other. The boats are long and narrow with shallow draft for getting up small streams. They have a small motor and a long drive shaft. Yesterday M had said we could walk around the rapids while the porters motored the boats up the rapids. I was facing forwards and suddenly Mukhtar's boat took off under motor followed by mine. What just happened? I had no way to communicate quickly with M and not enough Indonesian to communicate quickly with the porters in my boat.

Day one in the jungle and I can no longer call this a human powered trip. My trip will have an asterisk beside it an almost, a modification… I was too slow to react as I really did not know what to do. We had porters lined up at the other side of the trek. In hindsight, I should have just called 'stop'. I should have also recognized it as a sign that we were not communicating as clearly as I thought we were. Asking about other misunderstandings may have also helped avoid another major miscommunication that would soon have significant consequences for our plans.

We motored for two hours. It was fun weaving through small rapids and around logs. The boat rolls but corrects quickly so I got used to it. Overhead canopies of bamboo stretch out 40'-50' high in places. We had to get out and push a few times and to man-handle the boats up some small rapids and through blockages.

Hanbury-Tennison had previously described a similar experience in Borneo: "The river was narrow, with trees meeting overhead and lianas trailing in the water" (Hanbury-Tennison, 2017, p.42). Like Hanbury-Tennison's group

> We all fell under the spell of the forest. It is overwhelmingly luxuriant, a noisy cacophony of sound and endless variations of green. Mystery lurks behind the foliage: an infinity of undiscovered teeming life; plants, animals and insects new to science, waiting to be discovered. (Hanbury-Tennison, 2017, p.90)

We turned up a side tributary. The boatmen/porters finally dropped us in a small clearing that had been used as a camp. The plan was for them to motor up the main river (Sungai Bulu) another 2 hours while Mukhtar and I would trek through the jungle bypassing some rapids that we would not have been able to paddle up. I was ambivalent at this stage, feeling like the day was already ruined by the powered boat ride but M said he was cold from the river and preferred to walk, and he seemed confident he could find the trail. We would soon find out how disused some of the trails were becoming. *We split into two groups, the boatmen motoring upstream on the Sungai Bulu and with Mukhtar and I heading into the jungle across country.*

Mukhtar has an amazing memory for the jungle; even so, a lot had changed in the jungle in 5 years. *M and I spent 2.5 hours trying to find the trail up the mountain after we had hiked up a side stream a bit. By now it was getting dark and so we headed back towards the main river hoping that the porters might return for us at the drop-off point after we didn't arrive in time. Working against this was the fact that navigating the river after dark would be more difficult, but we knew that the locals often boated after dark.*

We finally connected on the radio one hour before dark. With more directions from the porters, we discussed the possibility of us hiking [towards the camp of the porters] *after dark. I was not keen on that idea, partly because our overconfidence in our estimated 1.5 hours hike had already turned into 2.5 hours of searching for the trail even in daylight. I discouraged a night hike. We have arranged to re-connect with the Long Layu porters in the morning.*

We spent a rough night in a rough camp since we had sent most of our food and dry gear upriver in the boat. It reminded me of my first night camping out in the Blue Mountains west of Sydney.

In the Australian Blue Mountains, my hiking partners and I had drifted off an old, disused trail and spent a rainy night in the bottom of a gully. I tried to sleep on a slope but kept sliding downhill into a hole we had dug for a fire-pit. The pit filled with rain. The next day we found our way out but had another cold night out in the mountains. There were 1½ inches of ice in the billy-can when we woke up. I was hooked on adventure from that point on.

On the ground there is an old rotted blue tarp someone has used in the past for shelter. We strung that up as a partial defense against the inevitable rain that evening. We spent several hours trying to fan a reluctant fire to dry our clothes a little. We shared a little rice and an egg for dinner. I tried all the tricks I could muster for staying warm. I had some spare clothes, so I slept in my hiking clothes and the spare T-shirt and shorts I was carrying. I wore a cap and wrapped my feet in a plastic bag since my socks were still wet.

Steve Camkin

I wrapped myself, cocoon-like in M's space blanket as much as I could while Mukhtar used my sleeping bag.

The ground is hard. I sleep very intermittently. I am still trying to figure out why we had motored up and that has me still a little miffed. Did M not clearly understand what the porters meant by walk around the rapids or how much motoring there was? I realize I am not very clear on how much of this area M traveled before. Did the porters not understand the importance to me, of completing the trip under human power?

I had time to think back over Day 1, which had not had an auspicious start. Motoring instead of paddling right at the start :(. When, the porters were showing us the start of the trail they pointed at a log bridge about 12 feet above the creek. It brought back memories of the obstacle courses I had tackled in the Army. In fact, our unit held the record for the fastest time. It looked a bit slippery but ok. Still, I balked, not feeling super-confident, and not wanting to take a chance so early in the trip. I weighed the balance of risk vs. reward. I did not see much of an upside to going across the log bridge; if I slipped and broke an ankle the trip would be over for me before it started.

Mukhtar decided to show me an alternate way down into the creek and took an 8-foot slide. Not inspiring!— I would soon be humbled myself. Early in the journey, I was skidding or butt-sliding down muddy banks; later I would find my balance and get better at negotiating the muddy slopes. However, I would never match the confidence of Mukhtar and the porters even when they were heavily laden. Climbing up the other side of a gully often required either a running start or using tree roots as foot or handholds. *We had then headed up the side creek that we thought would lead us, after several hours, to our first camp, couldn't't make sense of the terrain and had to backtrack. And now here we were!*

On Day 1 we had spent 2.5 hours hiking (plus the boating) for nearly zero progress towards our destination. I knew this was never going to be a trip with a meticulously planned itinerary with exactly calculated mileages and stopping points known in advance each day. We would be "checking in" each evening to sleep under a blue tarp, not a hotel.

> » *How do you respond when something you thought you had carefully planned, gets off to a rocky start?*

DECEMBER 17TH, 2019
Bush camp Sungai Bulu (Pa Ameb area) to bush camp on the Sungai Bulu (Pa Mut area)

Up early and broke camp. 20 minutes to get back to the first junction on the trail we had taken yesterday. Often to move forwards, you first have to move backwards.

The plan is for the porters to walk back to find us while we move towards them. Mukhtar is unsure of the way and asks if I want to climb the gunung [hill] in front of us and try to meet them as they come down. There is also a much easier ridge further right, which I suspect might be the way so I say "let's wait" so we don't pass them. The ridge to the right is where we finally connect with the porters. From there it is two hours to where the porters had set a very comfortable camp. There is a platform for sleeping, a big blue tarp, tons of firewood. We stop there for breakfast—tinned meat and rice. Porters started a fire using wood curls. After breakfast the trail was generally easier to follow—from here as it gets more foot traffic. The earlier section is rarely walked; mostly it is used by hunting groups. Rather than thinking of trails as a single linear solution to get from A to B, in Borneo it makes more sense to think of them like a spider web of connected routes. Some of the strands are stronger and clearer than others because they connect more important places or resources; others may be in a state of temporary disuse, unmaintained until there is a need to use them.

» *What historical paths, knowledge, or stories are falling into disuse in your organization or family?*

» *Are there some that should just be forgotten?*

» *Are there others that should be remembered?*

» *What is the difference between those that should be remembered and those that should be forgotten?*

Things seen today- two very small Gahuru trees, a pig's nest, a sow about 220 pounds across the river. Ate some wild ginger (jahe liar) and Umbud, a white starchy root. Drank from a vine that we slashed open with a parang.

The porters said I was "steady". Passed an old paddy field and an old Dyak cemetery across the river. Heard some Hornbills.

There are 13 kinds of Hornbills in Indonesia; several species are now very rare or critically endangered following extensive hunting and loss of habitat. One online source notes that Red Helmeted Hornbill beaks can be bought by dealers and sold for $1000 (Ingram, 2015). Brains, or the keratin in their beaks, are ground up for Chinese medicine or occasionally used in decorative carvings or beads. The species we saw were not endangered but are uncommon outside the deep forest. Hornbills have a distinctive, whoop, whoop, whoop sound as they flap overhead and they are an important part of Dyak cultural life. O'Hanlon (1987) describes his first encounter with the enchanting birds:

> The two great birds, larger than swans, four feet across the wings, flew heavily over the river, unperturbed…Their long tail plumes trailing, their wings making a whopping noise with each stroke, they alternatively flapped and sailed, laboring and gliding into the topmost branches of a dead tree on the far bank. (p.54)

ENERGY SUCKERS

A few more leeches (lintah), today after encountering the first ones yesterday. Some things are more irritating than other things. People often think of mosquitoes (nyamuk) and malaria when they think of the jungle. Mukhtar and I were in the higher elevations and did not encounter too many mosquitoes. Sand-flies (lilac pasir) were another story. They do not have the irritating drone of mosquitoes; they are smaller, seem to sneak through netting, and bite silently. Several times in other parts of Borneo they swarmed en masse forcing me to run or bike hard to get away.

Not many people have positive things to say about leeches. I was still getting rid of a few particularly persistent leech marks even several months later after returning home from Borneo. The Dyak and Penan invariably chop them in two with their parang. Leeches are, however, good models for being opportunistic. They conserve energy until an opportunity comes along. They are flexible and are wired to seek out opportunities (by sensing heat). When leeches do find a target, they move quickly. They can survive and even thrive in landscapes that many competitors avoid. You can try to protect yourself from leeches by staying out of their territory, by lathering on repellent which invariably gets sweated off, or by wearing long pants, long sleeves, and either long football socks or "leech socks". Sooner or later if you are in the jungle, they will find you. Ways to remove them include rolling them in a ball and flicking them off, scraping them off with a wooden stick, or applying salt, tobacco, or insect repellent. Leeches are more of a nuisance than a real threat. For some people, they are more of a drain on psychological energy.

» *What saps your energy?*

» *How do you mitigate the impact 'leeches' have on your life?*

Bathed in the river but I think I came out dirtier. Got hit with rain, which was quite chilly for a while. More tinned meat and rice for dinner. More rain today and in the evening. The rain hisses and splatter on the tarp and I drift off to sleep.

Steve Camkin

River Camp Sungai Bulu (Pa Ameb area) to Hillside Camp—"the camp where we had our last good meal" (Batu Ning area)

Hummock was nice to sleep in last night. I woke early to the sounds of jungle wildlife. At times the music was mad and chaotic, a discordant cacophony of a poorly coordinated orchestra. Cicadas, frogs, toads, gibbons, and birds all joined together. It seemed like every animal was intent on gaining fame in Borneo's Got Talent. The most common birds we heard were woodpeckers. The Gibbons' whoop whoop had a distinctive bass note.

We started the day with a river crossing then down into, and up out of, lots of steep gullies with muddy sides.

Lots of downed timber to scramble over or around. The porters disappeared quickly into the jungle, but I invariably located them again after rounding another bend in the terrain or a downed tree. *More Rattan* [vines] *to catch and hold you.*

I have encountered a similar plant in the North Queensland jungle of Australia. It is called the "Wait-a-While" vine because the vines hold you up with their sharp hooks. These vines seek out open areas including the edge of trails. The barbed wire of the Wait-a-While vines would scratch at my clothes, face, and arms if I was not careful or observant. Rattan is an extremely useful jungle resource though; it is used for lashings and furniture as well as for food. "Many species of Rattan can be eaten but not all" (Hansen, p.72). The mato tagara Rattan can cause your throat to swell up cutting off your air supply.

If I said the trail was getting easier I take that back. We stopped a number of times to re-find the trail. That day we followed the banks of the Sungai Bulu upstream. Sungai is the Indonesian word for river.

We stopped at Batu Pingal an overhanging rock near an old settlement on the Sungai Bulu. One of the porters' grandfathers had settled that area first. This was also the site where a local dance troup filmed a documentary detailing stories from the area. There is no settlement here anymore. Mukhtar and I had met one of the local dancers on our last night in Long Layu.

In recent years people have migrated up and down the rivers in the region for schools and medical facilities. This migration pattern has been occurring over hundreds of years although earlier migrations were usually related to the use of forest resources or social conflicts. Hansen notes that round trips from the Apokayan region might take 2-3 months (1988, p.201) on foot or by boat. I heard stories of round trips of five or six months to distant coastal towns for trading. Pelton (2007) describes a five-month trek that one of his guides made multiple times from the interior to the coast to trade where "...each man would carry 100 pounds" (p.113). Later in this journey, I would learn that on standard three-week military patrols the Indonesian soldiers would also carry 100 pounds off-trail through very rough terrain.

Lots of climbing today to get to the top of the range. Noticed more big trees today. Mukhtar's knee is playing up on him so he is walking a little slower. Ran out of tinned meat so we had rice and sweet ketsup, Ketsup Manis, for lunch...black and like treacle. I enjoyed it. Ate a raw birds egg that one of the porters found. The porters tried to shoot a pig today but two of the cartridges misfired. We had several other sightings but the pigs took off quickly.

Prior to increasing deforestation, there were infrequent but massive migrations by wild pigs over hundreds of miles. These migrations were dependent on infrequent heavy crops of seeds from *Dipterocarpaceae* (very tall, straight trees) and oaks (Hansen, 1988, p.130). Wild pig is still a food prized by the Dyak; they are hunted with spear, rifle, and dogs. Hansen (1988, p.79, 102) has a picture of a Penan native with a pig over 300 pounds that a Penan man carried solo on his back for half a mile.

One of the porters pointed out Honey-bear or Sun-Bear (berjemur) claw marks on a tree. The smallest of the bears, they are stocky and excellent climbers with a flattened chest, powerful forelimbs, and inward turned large claws as adaptations for climbing. Puri (2005, p.359) notes that "Sun-Bears are temperamental, irritable and brave. They will drop from high up in trees to get away from enemies." Illegal hunting, the wildlife trade, and deforestation are key threats to populations of Sun-Bears which are now listed as vulnerable by the IUCN (International Union for Conservation of Nature).

Earlier today, at a flat alongside a small creek we saw a tree that one of the porter's grandfathers had cut down at about three meters off the ground with a stone adze. The tree was 4 meters in diameter at the base and contained a Hornbill's nest. He wanted to gather the bird's feathers for a ceremonial headdress. The amount of effort used to cut down a tree of that size with a stone adze must have been amazing but ceremonies connected with the Hornbill have a very central place in Dyak culture.

Times are changing quickly in Borneo. In the last few centuries, the formerly nomadic Penan have traded items from the jungle such as rattan, damar gum, bezoar stone, and animal products through Kayan Dyak intermediaries to Chinese traders in downstream cities. In return, they may receive items such as shotgun shells, outboard motors, or iron tools. This pattern is also shifting as the Penan lifestyle has moved towards a more settled way of life. The Penan particularly, and also the Dyak, continue to rely upon their hunting and survival skills "…today despite pressures to settle down, become full-time farmers, and participate in Indonesia's development and conservation programs" (Puri, 2005, p.287).

Again, amazing to watch how quickly our porters set up camp. Poles for hummocks, firewood and fire, clearing vegetation etc. One of the porters went out hunting and came back with a Mouse deer (kancil) so it is Venison Shish Kabobs for dinner. He took the shot from 60 feet. He came back without the deer's head but with the deer's body partially dressed. Back at camp he finished butchering the animal on a bed of big leaves. We hiked 6 hours today.

Rained heavily today around 2:30 for about 90 minutes and again at about 7 pm. Camp is on a hillside on a moderately steep slope. There is a small rivulet close by but not big enough for washing in. Rain is splashing in or drifting in under the tarp even though I am 4 feet back from the edge of the tarp. The rain keeps drumming on the tarp for several hours. A civet cat (musang) stalks around camp. Some species of civet are regarded as pests because they kill chickens. The Malay Civet's "mournful cry at night is often mistakenly thought to be the sound of human ghosts wandering the forest" (Puri, 2005, p.361). *We are all huddled under one large tarp. I am quite toasty warm but some bugs manage to find me. I sleep on the ground on a tarp, sleeping bag and liner sheet. I have some more chunks of roast Mouse Deer and gradually drift off to sleep.*

DECEMBER 19TH, 2019
Hillside Camp (Batu Ning area)
to Durian Tree Camp (Night 1)

I woke up to dried blood. A leech managed to get me in the neck last night. Tea, rice, and deer meat for breakfast. Heard more deer barking at breakfast time. The civet has made off with some of the Mouse Deer meat.

It seemed like a slow pack-up today. We hiked 1.5 hours today. Headed down a moderately steep spur then sidled around multiple drainages. Steep gullies with muddy banks to climb in and out of. Hard work, tricky footing. One of our porters found some tree resin (damar gum) along the way for fire-starting.

Damar gum is now a "valued ingredient in eco-paints, as it is completely non-toxic" (Hanbury-Tennison, 2014, p.71).

We passed one small campsite but I think we were off trail most of the time. Emerson said: "Do not go where the path may lead; go instead where there is no path and make a trail". We certainly were doing just that. *Finally down another steep spur to a small side creek where we found the site of either a temporary camp or a small abandoned kampong.* In territory that is new to us sometimes we can follow a trail left by others, and sometimes we must find our own way. There is an Australian Aboriginal proverb: "Traveler, there are no paths. Paths are made by walking".

There is a large old Durian tree but no fruit. Durian is common in Indonesia and in fruit season is an abundant food source. Durian tastes a bit like custard, but it smells so bad (like dirty socks or rotten food) that many hotels in Asia prohibit customers from bringing it into hotel rooms. I usually eat it while pinching my nostrils so as not to smell it.

In June 2020 a mysterious package caused six German postal workers to be hospitalized and six others to be treated for nausea. The building where they worked was evacuated. The package turned out to be a box of over-ripe Durian (Picheta & Pleiten 2020). It was not the first time Durian was responsible for evacuations. An Indonesian plane (2018), the Royal Melbourne Institute of Technology (RMIT) (2018), and the University of Canberra (2019) have all been evacuated due to suspected gas leaks. All were later attributed to rotting Durian fruit (Jones, 2020).

The news is not all bad though. Several universities around the world have been exploring "...the benefits of finding a green use for durian's headline-making, stomach-churning waste as over 70% of the fruit tends to be thrown away" (Jones, 2020). Specifically, the universities are assessing whether inedible parts of Durian or Jackfruit, another common forest fruit, "...could provide the material to make a new generation of super-capacitors that can charge mobile phones, tablets and laptops within minutes" (Jones, 2020).

There is a clearing about 20 x 40', some old vertical poles, and lots of other old poles and fire-wood on the ground. I am struck by the fact that this old timber will quickly be recycled by the forest. In more modern villages across Indonesia, there are significant problems with rubbish disposal since there is no real trash collection and many modern items are not recyclable. Trash is often burned or swept into ditches or creeks. Later in our travels downriver Mukhtar and I would pass a number of towns that have introduced plans to address this issue.

There is also a big dead tree close to the tarp so we have discussions on which way to run (lari!) if it should come down. Redmond O'Hanlon, while being briefed for his journey, was warned of the hazards of tree-fall. "Check the tree trunks for termites. Termites mean dead branches and dead branches, sooner or later, mean dead men. We lost a lot of men like that" (O'Hanlon, 1987, pp. 3-4).

Mukhtar builds a small fire (api) for some tea (te) and I wash my clothes just in time for the sun to disappear. The sun was out for 15 minutes with moderate strength but now is like weak tea. I even saw my shadow for the first time in 4 days. Typical late wet season cloud cover.

I am still thinking about how we can re-do the first river section that we used motors for, but this time just by paddling or hiking. Mukhtar offers some suggestions. He is a consummate problem-solver. We heard people with chainsaws and no boat on Day 1 of the trek so he thinks they must have walked. Not sure why this option of hiking was not clearer when we departed—but at least it opens up the possibility of a return trip at a later date. We would boat up the river and hike back to Long Layu.

I had not really been watching what was going on with the others as I was exploring the area and taking photos. So, I was surprised when I learned that the porters were about to leave. I had been expecting a "hand-off" between the two groups of porters, although we had discussed the possibility that we may need to wait in the jungle for the Apauping porters. We are assured that the other group will be arriving soon, and we are told that we should wait there until they arrive. I wish the porters a safe trip back and thank them for bringing us this far and showing me some of their jungle skills.

The porters have left us with camp set up and are heading back to Long Layu which they will do in one day. They will probably hunt for pig along the way. The porters are eager to get back as they are on the Christmas committee for Long Layu.

Having the porters leave us here was a bit of a surprise! At this point we are not quite sure when the porters will be here from Apauping (a village of about 600 people). Kind of expected some of the waiting games in Borneo. I thought we had coordinated a pickup date before we left Long Layu but there was a chance we would need to wait until the porters from Apauping arrived.

I am surprised how cool it is in the forest when it is raining. We are in the highlands but the elevation is not that great. My high-school schoolbook's description of the jungle was not accurate. The jungle floor [here] *is not generally clear but has lots of tangled vegetation. Maybe the Amazon jungle is different. Also, the rivers are muddier here than the clear streams I saw while trekking in the North Queensland jungle. The jungle is not just big tall trees* but a mixture of layers which can make visibility and travel a challenge at times. *Not many mosquitoes. Heard another Hornbill flying overhead with its distinctive flapping sound and call.*

Under the tarp now in dry clothes. Trying to keep my feet as dry as possible. One set of wet, dirty clothes goes on in the morning; dry shorts, synthetic t-shirt and flip-flops go on at evening. Amongst the advice passed along by those who have traveled extensively in the Borneo jungle is "…get up at 5.30 and into your wet kit. It's uncomfortable at first, but don't weaken-ever; if you do, there'll be two sets of wet kit in no time, you'll lose sleep and lose strength and then there'll be a disaster" (O'Hanlon, 1987, pp. 5-6).

Listening to some gibbons (siamang). We detect "…the whooping call, the owl-like, clear, ringing hoot of the female Borneo gibbon" (O'Hanlon, 1987, p.42).

Had a lunch of rice, deer meat and lemon tea at 1:30. We have about two and half pounds of rice and some sachets of coffee and spices. We are expecting the new porters to bring more food but now I am little uneasy about the fact that the Long Layu porters have taken the rest of the food back. It seemed like a reasonable decision at the time since more food was coming and we did not want to be carrying a lot of extra weight. *Unlikely we will move from here today unless the Apauping porters arrive by 2pm. By mid to late afternoon confusion starts to build. Time drifts on and the porters from Apauping have not arrived yet.*

A text from my dear friend I had received earlier back in Long Layu had read "You are going to meet someone else in the jungle? Hmmm". Sometimes people on the outside can sense things we cannot. We started pondering 'what if' scenarios. 'What is our plan if the Apauping porters do not arrive?' *Mukhtar says it is easy to follow the river downstream from here but if there are only two of us to move downstream and if one of us gets injured, it could be a minor epic.* By late afternoon I am *feeling slightly feverish. Yesterday and today's exposure to alternating cold and heat? Could it be from minor wounds, infections and bites?*

I asked Mukhtar to share some stories while we wait for the porters from Apauping to arrive. *Near the Busang River Mukhtar* related that he had seen *a shadow moving very fast through the forest. He saw a small footprint on the rock and then another. Penan in the jungle. Another time in 1986 he met a Penan wearing a bark loincloth.* On reflection, some of my comments sound culturally insensitive but they come from a place of admiration. I had spent some time with the Penan in Sarawak, Malaysia a few years earlier and been incredibly impressed by their bushcraft skills and their ability to make the most of the resources in the jungle environment. *Mukhtar mentioned some Dyak still living in caves. He has seen, many years ago, very old Chinese porcelain jars near Long Saan on our future route but he thinks they have been "collected" now. There might be some still left in Jelet* another future destination.

If the rivers were previously the main transport avenues, the jungle trails were secondary roads. Aircraft, roads, and outboard motors have now changed the trade patterns. Museum exhibits and books, I had read (Hansen, p.144) shared similar stories of items like sewing machines and boat engines being carried for weeks or months from the large coastal towns hundreds of miles inland on the backs of porters negotiating narrow, slippery jungle trails. Elsewhere in Borneo, I had heard tales of trading voyages hundreds of miles long and months in duration where boats carved from hardwood had been dragged and pushed upriver across jungle-clad ranges and down through wild rapids on the other side. The ordeal was then repeated in reverse. Later in our trip, Mukhtar told me of a specialized group of people known for their physique-hewn from a lifetime of paddling large trading canoes upriver. Their craft lasted until a few generations ago when small motors were introduced.

Mukhtar told me stories about some of the other villages in the region. *Long Saan was abandoned in 1969. Setulang was settled by Long Saan people who left after a big fight between Long Saan and Jelet youth. Long Saan people left to go downriver, stopped to harvest, crossed the mountains and headed towards Malinau. They built another boat and moved to the site now called Setulang.*

Time is now 5pm just before dark in the forest. No sign of the Apauping porters yet. Drank some coffee, washed in the stream (good to feel clean!) and waiting for the deer soup that we made from some left-over bones to boil. Mukhtar is getting anxious [me too!] that the porters are not going to show up and that the Long Layu porters took most of the food with them. We are concerned the porters on both sides may have mis-communicated about the meeting point despite apparent multiple earlier conversations on the location. *We are at an old kampong site* we thought! *but I wonder if there could be more than one old kampong site?*

One of the dilemmas faced in survival situations is whether to stay put and wait for rescue or whether to try to self-rescue. While the general advice from search and rescue experts is to stay put, some circumstances warrant an exception. Juliane Koepcke would not have been seen from the air through the jungle canopy; no one from the plane crash mentioned in *Miracle in the Andes* (Parrado & Rause, 2006), would have survived if someone had not finally walked out braving avalanches, cold and steep slopes.

A jungle question for you:

          Steve Camkin

» *What would you do?*

» *Sit and wait for a response from Long Layu or Apauping when porters do not show up on time?*

» *Try to walk the two and a half days back to Long Layu on our own?*

» *Try to walk out alone to Apauping, our planned destination?*

» *Try to call the Long Layu porters on the radio?*

4

DECIDING

*"The last of human freedoms is ones ability to choose
one's attitude in a given set of circumstances."*

VIKTOR FRANKL

Durian Tree Camp (Night 2)

*A waiting day. Killing time to see if the porters from Apauping
will show up today. Mukhtar does some short trips circling
around the camp trying to find any sign of the trail towards
Apauping. He yells out periodically and I yell back so he can
find his way back to camp. I try to keep a fire stoked and pile
green leaves on periodically in case the smoke helps the Apauping porters to find us. It's not very effective though, the smoke
scatters in the high tree canopy overhead.*

Our brains do not like uncertainty or conditions outside of
normal routine. In its attempts to conserve energy our brains create
routines or templates from which to operate. These templates or
files are stored in our subconscious and are used to run most of our
daily operations—functions like breathing, routine administrative
tasks, or driving the same route to work each day. When the brain

encounters new situations or tasks, we often become disoriented and the brain is forced to work harder to make sense of the experience and new templates for action—if X happens do Y. New tasks and new situations are more stressful and more tiring, mentally, physically, and emotionally.

>> *How can you manage yourself during a disorientation phase?*

>> *How can you effectively analyze a situation in order to make sense of it and create a plan?*

>> *Perhaps you feel like you are already through the disorientation stage of a crisis. How you might help others who are still feeling disoriented?*

One caution though. Ocean waves come in series; rivers often have more than one set of rapids. Peter Vaill (1996) urges leaders to develop the capabilities to manage not just one wave of change, but to develop strategies for survival in a world of 'permanent whitewater'. Vaill sees learning as a way of being. Learning is a core competency for managing ongoing and constant change. The ability to learn is a necessity for survival and for individual and organizational growth. Wendell Phillips asks "What is defeat? Nothing but education; nothing but the first steps to something better" (https://www.brainyquote.com/quotes/wendell_phillips). In the technology industry in Silicon Valley "...start-ups don't launch with polished, finished businesses. Instead, they release their 'Minimum Viable Product' (MVP)—the most basic version of their core idea with only one or two essential features" (Holiday, 2014, p.82).

>> *How are you choosing to view setbacks?*

>> *What learning might you glean from them?*

There are a variety of tools we can use and questions we can ask ourselves to manage disorientation, to analyze a situation, and to start planning.

P.F.D. One simple tool I use in uncertain situations is P.F.D. A personal flotation device (P.F.D.) keeps us afloat when we are tossed into turbulent waters. It can also stand for Pause, Focus, and Decide. Pause—What is happening? Focus—What is most important? Decide—What action should I take or not take?

Let's think about "Pause" for the situation in which Mukhtar and I found ourselves. It was late afternoon on the day the porters from Long Layu left. We had an increasing realization that:

1. We were not in the agreed-upon meeting place.

2. The porters from Long Layu probably believed they had dropped us in the correct location, however, they were mistaken.

3. There was a chance (degree unknown) that our porters from Apauping might not find us at our present location.

4. We did not know what action if any, the porters from either location might take when we were overdue or when they might decide to take any action.

5. We had minimal food.

6. Others knew of our plans, but not our location. We thought it was likely that someone would start a search eventually, but we did not know when.

Mukhtar and I then switched to Focus. We assessed that there was no immediate threat we needed to react to. Our focus was now on making sure we did nothing stupid that would make things worse.

For the Decide stage, we first noted our immediate options and discussed the pros and cons of each. Should we:

a. *Try to quickly head back after the Long Layu porters?*

b. *Do nothing yet; construct a more detailed plan later?*

c. *Stay in place until someone comes for us?*

d. *Head off towards Apauping and perhaps connect with the Apauping porters along the way?*

A jungle question for you…

» *What would you do and why?*

S.T.O.P. (Stop, Think, Observe, Plan) is another tool that can help decision-making during a crisis. When our brain encounters a danger, it sends an immediate message to be on alert via a 'fast path'. This often translates first as a 'freeze' on action. Another message follows via a 'slow path' which is more rational and thoughtful. The amygdala, the emotional side of our brain, also helps by flooding our system with adrenaline to strengthen muscles. Problems can occur if we get stuck in a 'freeze' state and we are unable to choose the right action (Sherwood, 2009).

Survival experts advocate use of the S.T.O.P. framework (similar to P.F.D.) in risky scenarios (Gossamergear, 2019). The S stands for Stop, but it can also stand for stay in place; a reminder to consider the pros and cons of staying where you are versus moving on. One thing P.F.D and S.T.O.P. have in common is that they work to prevent fear and emotions from hijacking the brain's amygdala. Instead, they allow the more rational and thinking part of the brain, the neo-cortex, to guide action. The S.T.O.P. can be a few seconds or it can be longer depending on the demands of the situation and the types of risks encountered.

Both the P.F.D. and S.T.O.P. tools highlight the importance of observation and focus for assessing a situation. The location Mukhtar and I were in did not allow us an easy way to observe the world around us.

Our location contributed to a sense of uncertainty and ambiguity. It is hard to know how to adapt to changing situations when you cannot pick up signals on upcoming changes early enough. Our camp was located on the side of a hill at the head waters of a very small stream, down in a valley surrounded by layers of hills with tall trees towering over-head. It is easy to get disoriented when you cannot literally see the forest for the trees. A well-known African proverb though encourages travelers to "fear no forest because it is dense". A crisis or change is more difficult for people when they cannot see a way through.

When one is in a new situation or environment, knowing how to observe, to broaden our focus, and to interpret the presence of new information in our situation is an important survival and resilience skill. Many indigenous groups have a different way of looking at the world. Their perspective is partly based on different value systems, partly on how work is organized, and partly on the geography of where they live. There is an Australian aboriginal saying "We are all visitors to this time, this place. We are just passing through. Our purpose here is to observe, to learn, to grow, to love… and then we return home" (www.quotes.net).

An eye-tracking experiment by Richard Nisbett and others (Nisbett, Chua & Boland, 2005) at the University of Michigan found that

> …participants from East Asia tend to spend more time looking around the background of an image—working out the context whereas people in America tended to spend more time concentrating on the main focus of the picture… And by guiding our attention, this narrow or diverse focus directly determines what we remember at a later date." (Robson, 2017, p.8)

I have seen snow-climbers get themselves into survival situations because they were so focused on the next technical steps that they missed approaching adverse weather. The increase in 'selfie' deaths might be attributed partly to too much focus on the bigger picture and future notoriety and to distraction from necessary details and situational awareness (Lovitt, 2016). To survive and thrive we need to switch focus back and forth between the big picture and the details. To be resilient you have to first survive.

Robson (2020) suggests that our vision and perception can be influenced by our social and cultural lives:

> People in more collectivist societies tend to be more wholistic in the way they think about problems, focusing more on the relationships and the context of the situation at hand, while people in individualistic societies tend to focus on separate elements, and to consider situations as fixed and unchanging. (p.5)

These observations have implications not just for assessing a survival situation, but also for how we respond to challenges in our work or daily lives. John Kotter (1996) has pointed out that the effectiveness of change efforts is dependent not just on technical aspects, but on human factors and relational aspects. Leaders of change efforts helping organizations survive a crisis or stay resilient would do well to recognize and incorporate diverse perspectives of how people view those challenges.

» *How are you ensuring that you pay attention to both the big picture and the details?*

» *What do you tend to see or not see?*

During my trekking in Borneo, I tried several ways to be more present by listening and observing.

Listening. When we were in the jungle, I noticed that Mukhtar and the porters had exceptional listening skills. Their ability to pick up different animal calls or use sounds as an indicator of a changing landscape was impressive. Penan hunters use "...the noise of nearby streams, wind and rain ...to cover the sounds of an advancing hunter" (Puri, 2005, p.236). Mukhtar and the local porters often seemed to listen also for discernment or enjoyment. When Mukhtar shared stories with the locals he showed that same appreciative listening.

One listening framework is outlined in the Carlson Listening Styles survey (Wolvin & Coackley, 1996). The styles are:

- Appreciative listening. Listening for enjoyment.

- Empathic listening. Listening to put yourself in the other person's shoes.

- Discerning listening. Listening to make sure you get all the information.

- Comprehensive listening. Listening to understand thoughts, ideas, or a message.

- Evaluative listening. Listening to assess something.

Different listening styles are suited for different situations; however, we often rely on just one or two.

Listening effectively can help to gather information about the environment we are operating in, concerns that people have about changes, or to appreciate things that are going well before celebrating small wins.

» *What are you listening for?*

» *Who else and what else should you be listening to or for?*

Silence is rare in the jungle. When it happens, it may signal something is awry. Silence can also signify many things in business and personal relationships. Lawrence Durrell writes in *Justine*, "Does not everything depend on our interpretation of the silence around us?" An Arapaho saying states "All plants are our brothers and sisters. They talk to us and if we listen, we can hear them".

» *How often are you listening just to your own voice?*

» *How can you practice the five listening styles?*

» *What are people 'saying' by their silence?*

Observation. Observation is another skill that helps us to anticipate or react to changes in our environment. Marcel Proust says in *'La Prisonnière'*, the fifth volume of 'Remembrance of Things Past' "the real voyage of discovery consists not in seeking new lands but in seeing with new eyes."

Indigenous hunting skills depend not just on the action part of hunting, but on deep skills of observation and perception.

For many tribal peoples, continuous immersion in nature over thousands of years has resulted in a profound attunement to the subtle cues of the natural world. Acute observations have taught tribes how to hunt wild game and gather roots and berries, how to sense changes in climate, predict movements of ice sheets, the return of migrating geese and the flowering seasons of fruit trees. Sophisticated hunting, tracking, husbandry and navigation techniques have also been the ingenious responses of tribal peoples to the challenges of varied, and often hostile, environments. The development of such observations and skills is not only testament to the latent creativity of humans and their extraordinary ability to adapt but has also ensured that when living on their lands, employing the techniques they have honed over generations, tribal peoples are typically healthy, self-sufficient and happy. (Eede, 2013)

As one Yanomami tribal member from the Amazon said: "I am the environment, I was born in the forest. I know it well" (Kopenawa, 2020, p.1).

Our perceptions are determined by the data our senses feed us concerning what we expect to see, feel, hear, touch, taste, and by what we 'know' and what we 'believe'. Perceptions are not photographs of reality, they are constructions or artworks—something that our minds create. This construction process has value in a survival situation. It helps us make sense of the world; it may also get us into trouble when those constructions are inaccurate.

Later during our trek Mukhtar and I climbed a rope and rattan ladder to get up the side of a cliff. Some of the rungs were broken, some were shaky. Later, reflecting on the experience, it brought to mind the concept of the 'Ladder of Inference' articulated by Argyris (1990). It is a succinct description of the way we observe, selectively pick data, and then draw inferences and conclusions from it. Challenging our own observation processes can be a valuable tool to help us examine the reality or construction of our world. Survivors are often those who can, after encountering disorientation, create the most accurate representation of their new world and deal with its realities.

> *What biases might you have in what you choose to observe and how you interpret events?*

The role of leaders as meaning makers, helping identify opportunities and threats in the environment, becomes even more important in times of ambiguity and when organizations are navigating new territory. Leaders cannot make sense of what is going on around them if they are constantly focused just on action. Today one of the needed skills of leaders is to know when to stop, listen, and observe.

Observing is only part of the process of anticipation and

adaptation though; creating a language to share the observations is another aspect. Language both represents how we see the world and shapes how we operate in our environment.

In the Penan language there are forty words for sago palm, and no words for goodbye, or thank you – or thief. The Penan are a nomadic people who view the entire rainforest as their home. They are an "Eco-village" on the move, one with a history many thousands of years old. (Davis, 1991, p.48).

Until the 1960s the Penan people lived as nomads, communicating with different groups when on the move in the rainforest through a complex signal system of stick and leaf symbols they call *oroo*. *Oroo* relayed such messages as the person passing here was unwell, or the person who passed here was hungry (Davis, 1991, p.6).

The environment the Penan and the Dyak peoples operate in has shaped their languages. Hansen describes message sticks that were left for him, by Penan, during his travels. "They were four feet long and stuck obliquely into the ground. Notches and clefts along the sticks were embellished with pieces of Rattan, leaves and twigs (p.75)." Penan near Long Kerong had shown me, on one of my previous trips to Borneo, how they left signals just by bending leaves, an even more subtle form of communication.

Later, Mukhtar and I saw some stick signals used by Dyak people in the area to communicate with others passing by. The porters from Apauping also left us some very obvious oroo indicating the direction that we should travel. It seemed that they had sensed that we would appreciate clear, unambiguous signs given the condition we were likely in.

The Penan, Dyak, and Lun Dayeh are adept at reading natural signs indicating changes in their environment. Penan hunters follow solitary male Bearded Pigs in the forest. The pigs follow large flocks of Flying Foxes which follow swarms of migratory bees that are searching for flowers from fruit trees. The pigs feed on the forest fruits. Solitary male pigs are followed by large herds of migrating pigs (Puri, 2005, p.255).

Steve Camkin

» *What signs about upcoming change might you miss because of poor observational skills?*

» *Employees in companies actually speak many 'languages'- finance, engineering, HR, marketing, Executive, Mid-level Manager, Front Line Worker— what are you missing because you do not speak other languages?*

» *What can you do to understand and to better speak other languages?*

Reconnaissance. Reconnaissance is a structured form and extension of observation skills. Mukhtar and I used 'reconnaissance' to gather more information to try to solve the questions of Where are we? What resources do we have in the area? And what paths could we take from here? First, we tried small forays in the immediate vicinity to see if we could find either our trail back to Long Layu or another trail going forward to Apauping. Once Mukhtar and I decided to stay temporarily in place, we kept extending our reconnaissance efforts further afield, focusing on trying to find the 'trail' we had come in on. At times this looked promising, but eventually, these leads proved useless.

'Trails' in this region are not how they are in more densely populated regions. We were really looking for off-trail signs like crushed vegetation or the occasional cut mark on a tree. We zigzagged across the complicated landscape trying to find the trail back. We realized that our porters had made sufficient marks to get us where we were, but they were insufficient for us to follow our trail back. Part of the problem was that heavy rain had obliterated much of the sign. One mistake I made was that I had not been paying enough attention to where I was going. My focus had been on enjoying the jungle and on moving quickly and safely. I had been eager to prove my competence to others.

Marking a trail. There are times when leaders are expected to lead.

> » *When you are 'marking the way' for others (employees, colleagues, children) are you leaving a clear trail, especially if people are new to a situation or task?*

> » *What signs are you leaving that might be helpful to people?*

> » *How long will your trail last if you do not keep leaving signs or don't make the signposts clear enough?*

> » *What is lost if you only focus on the future and do not pay attention to where you are or have been?*

> » *Rather than blazing your own trail—has anyone before been where you are going?*

S.W.O.T. Another way to make sense of a situation is to inventory what you see as Strengths, Weaknesses, Opportunities, and Threats of the situation. Looking back at the situation Mukhtar and I found ourselves in, our inventory at the time included:

STRENGTHS

- We were both physically fit with no known medical issues.
- We both had experience living and trekking in the jungle although Mukhtar's experience was much deeper than mine.
- There was plenty of water around.
- We had camping gear with us.

WEAKNESSES

- We did not know our exact location.

- We did not have much food.

- We did not have an effective means of communicating with the porters or with the outside world.

OPPORTUNITIES

- With Mukhtar's knowledge of the jungle, there were opportunities to supplement our food.

- The jungle provided additional resources for water, fire, and camping.

THREATS

- Injury. My biggest concern was that there were only two of us. I was confident we could find our way to a village or survive long enough for someone to find us. If one of us was injured though, by something even as minor as a twisted ankle, we would be in serious trouble.

- Exhaustion. With little food and (we anticipated) at least 2.5 days to hike out, getting tired was a recipe for a mistake or an injury.

- Steep terrain. Off-trail travel. Unknown route. Water hazards.

Doing a SWOT analysis helps in thinking through how to mitigate weaknesses and manage threats while leveraging strengths and preparing to take advantage of opportunities that arise. With food, for example, we rationed our existing supplies. We also took advantage of limited opportunities to gather food along the way, including fern tips, Rattan roots, and Buabarra fruits.

Transitions and Stop. Start. Continue. Another advantage of careful, ongoing observation is that it can help frame a very simple action plan for what adaptations one needs to make and what actions to stop, start, or continue. Mukhtar and I needed to stop eating all our food at once, start looking for other food and continue managing our energy to reduce calorie needs. Changing situations and changing directions implies transitions whether smooth or abrupt. In 'The First 90 Days' Watkins (2003) discusses common transitions that employees go through when changing jobs. Some of these are relevant to the experience Mukhtar and I had in transitioning from being victims of a situation to being survivors. Watkins counsels new managers to: take a mental break from the old job; match strategy to situations; secure early wins; achieve alignment; build your team; keep your balance; and see

Steve Camkin

the forest and the trees (pix). Mukhtar and I used most of these tactics as we focused on surviving.

Think of a current situation faced by you, your family, team, or organization.

> » *What do you need to Stop, Start, or Continue doing?*
>
> » *What transitions are you and the people around you going through?*
>
> » *What can you do to help yourself and others prepare for the next stage?*

Goodman, Schlossberg & Anderson (2006) developed the 4S model to help adults in transitions. They suggested examining four groupings of factors that influence a person's ability to manage personal transitions. In a transition situation, these factors can be used as a checklist to see what we may currently have some influence over or might be able to gain some influence over. The four groupings are:

- **Situation** (e.g., level of control, changing roles, duration, prior similar experiences, other stressors)

- **Self** (e.g., psychological resources, personal and demographic characteristics)

- **Support** (e.g., friends, family, networks, institutions, communities)

- **Strategies** (e.g., for modifying the situation, changing the meaning, managing stress)

While Goodman, Schlossberg & Anderson (2006) developed the model to help individuals, organizations could also use the 4S model as a framework for assessing or developing organizational resilience.

» *Are there aspects of these four areas that you could use to help you, or others, manage a transition?*

Strategic Thinking vs. Strategic Planning. Edward DeBono, an expert in creative thinking, argued that "...when you are pulling yourself out of a swamp, you do not consult a road map.... The objective is to escape from an uncomfortable position rather than to reach a particular destination" (De Bono,1981, p.89). That was the situation Mukhtar and I found ourselves in, figuratively, and also, on occasion literally. Our first and highest priority was to stay safe. Our second-highest priority was to either make contact with others in the forest or reach a settled area; it did not really matter which area.

The way we think about our world guides our actions in the world. It makes sense to periodically test our assumptions about the world, especially during times of change. The model of organizations as machines is based on seeing the world as being predictable. Kanyi's (2011) interpretation of Mintzberg's work is that Mintzberg pointed out the fallacy of predictability, the shrinking of planning horizons, and the limitations of traditional strategic planning in disruptive environments. In the jungle the planning horizon that Mukhtar and I had was limited at times to a few feet; other times we could see further, but the direction was unclear. Sometimes emerging barriers such as rapids and cliffs threatened to block our progress.

Mintzberg suggests that "strategic planning is about analysis while strategic thinking is about synthesis. Strategic planning in this case means breaking down a goal into steps, designing how the steps may be implemented, and estimating the anticipated consequences of each step while strategic thinking is about using intuition and creativity to formulate an integrated perspective, a vision, of where the organization should be heading (Kanyi, 2011). The ambiguity of our situation in the jungle, and our limited ability to gather additional data meant that Mukhtar and I needed to use a strategic thinking approach to our situation.

Steve Camkin

"In practical terms strategic thinking should help to analyze, explore, understand and define a complex situation and then develop planning actions that will bring the greatest possible positive impact towards a pre- defined goal..." (Kanyi, 2011). Mukhtar and I had several pre-defined goals but attempting to tightly define and quantify dozens of linear steps would have been an exercise in wasted energy and increased frustration. We needed to adapt rather than dominate.

Another definition describes strategic planning as

> ...a linear process and set of steps where there are a defined start and end and multiple short-term goals. ...It also encompasses both traditional and logical ways of thinking and typically involves analyzing data and defining a goal. But does this process always end in favorable results? Not so much in today's increasingly uncertain business climate. Strategic thinking is a more fluid concept that is not so linear and instead encourages creativity, investigation, and in tuition in the decision-making process. It allows us to be more adaptable where planning is not practical...Unique and innovative strategic thinking which aligns with a company's goals and vision will help them stay competitive. (Inscape, 2017)

For Mukhtar and me staying competitive in the jungle meant staying alive and increasing our chances of being rescued or making our way out. Sharing ideas, asking questions, staying flexible, and thinking outside of the 'data box' were some of the strategic thinking skills that we applied. Traditional strategic planning works when you can extrapolate. It works far less well in disrupted environments.

> » *Does your organization need strategic planning or strategic thinking now?*

>> *What is the right balance between planning and adapting?*

Prospect Theory. Prospect Theory (Kahneman & Tversky, 1979) suggests that people under stress will take either a gradual approach to work their way out of a tough situation, or they make a dramatic move. Often it is the latter, even though the risks are increased, and chances of success are lower. In one classic example, Fred Smith, the founder of FedEx, saved the company from bankruptcy when he gambled the last of company funds at the blackjack table (Zhang, 2014). Gonzales (2004) describes many cases where people needed to take significant risks that were sometimes counterintuitive or against the prevailing wisdom, in order to survive.

A jungle question for you-

>> *What would you do?*

>> *Return back to Long Layu (hopefully the shorter way along a more known path) or try to move forward to Apauping?*

>> *Stay where you are- stick with your strengths but risk failing to complete the objective?*

>> *Venture into the unknown, still in the direction you were planning on going anyway?*

When people are trying to reorient themselves, their teams, or their companies, here are some questions to consider.

>> *Is there a base your company needs to return to or do you need to move forward in a different direction?*

>> *What is stopping you from moving forward in your work?*

» *Does your team or company culture and strategy encourage a 360-degree perspective?*

» *Are you or your team "stuck" looking back to better times in the past?*

» *Is your team looking outwards at other industries?*

» *Is your team too focused on the future with no regard for learning from the past?*

Time. Time can be another form of disorientation. I felt the impact of time disorientation in the jungle, and I am feeling its impact during the COVID-19 epidemic, losing track of days and even weeks.

At times, I was puzzled by the slow pace that Mukhtar and I were making even on our way into our planned rendezvous site. There were delays in finding, and re-finding the trail, and diversions to chase down pigs for a possible meal. As the trip went on, I shifted my approach to time.

> People who are used to living in cities, where the streets and highways are set out in orderly fashion, have little regard for the proper pace of jungle travel. They are renowned for their lack of patience when it becomes impossible to walk in a straight line... [Like Hansen who preceded me] I began to learn that the only way to enjoy jungle travel was by remaining as flexible as possible in the face of the unavoidable, changing circumstances. (Hansen, 1988, p.132)

I never asked, in advance, the distance between Long Layu and Apauping. I had learned on earlier trips that the number of days was a more useful unit of measurement when trekking in the jungle; and to hold that loosely. I later learned the distance was about 40 miles. For someone used to hiking on broad well-maintained

Western trails our trek was painfully slow progress, but at the time it had seemed we were covering long distances each day.

In my consulting work, I often see organizations challenged by time. Some argue that speed is critical for organizational survival; others argue to slow things down so that catastrophic mistakes are avoided. Some employees are criticized for impractical futuristic ideas, while others are criticized for not learning from history. Margerison (1987) provides a framework and questions, using the concept of time for moving along stuck conversations. He envisions conversations along two axes. The vertical axis represents time. From top to bottom this is represented as Future, Present, and Past. The horizontal axis from left to right represents a focus on General or Specific. To shift a conversation, choose a question with a different time or specificity focus.

» *What have you learned from the past that might be relevant for the future?*

» *How can you apply general principles to specific issues you are facing?*

One of the things Mukhtar and I speculated at the time we were lost was that the porters from Long Layu and Apauping had different understandings of where the meeting place was. We were supposed to meet at a large grassy clearing at an old village site. Although a "large grassy clearing" is rare in the jungle, there might have been more than one location fitting this description. Since both groups were from different areas and the trail was getting increasingly disused, it seemed possible that the two groups were referring to different locations. They had different mental maps or models of the terrain. In planning my larger Borneo expedition, I had compared multiple maps of Borneo, both paper and digital, with differing scales and information. As adventurer Robert Young Pelton notes, "Every map tells a story and has a purpose...Each map shines a bit more light on this dark region (p.153)." A map is not the actual terrain; it is a representation of the terrain. Similarly, everyone has different mental maps or understandings of the world. Those maps are shaped by our past experiences, conscious and unconscious biases, what is important to us, and what is not. When Hansen's maps proved totally inadequate, his guides had shown him, using sticks and twigs on the ground, how they remembered the way. (Hansen, 1988) Whilst in the Australian Army I had used 'mud maps' as a teaching and briefing aid before an exercise.

The most detailed map Hansen had been able to find in the 1980s was an Operational Navigation Chart produced by the British Ministry of Defense at a scale of 1:1,000,000. In contrast, most modern hiking maps have a scale of 1:24,000. Hansen found that names of places were forty years out of date, the few surveyors had not agreed on their findings, the borders between Sarawak, Sabah and Kalimantan did not align and "...there were conspicuous white areas bordered by comments such as: "Map Sources irreconcilable" and "Limits of reliable relief information (p.61-62)." The fine print read "Reliability Warning: Owing to inadequate source material there may be significant positional discrepancies in detail over areas of this chart" (Hansen, 1988, p.62). O'Hanlon made similar comments on the available maps he had area un-surveyed, map sources unreliable, inadequate source material, relief data incomplete (O'Hanlon, 1987, p. 110).

What I found on this recent trek in Borneo was still surprisingly similar to Hansen's and O'Hanlon's experience: villages that no longer existed were still recorded; roads that had been planned but were never constructed were marked; roads that had been built were not marked. Google Earth maps are just a blur at the scale we would have needed for Western-style navigation. It would be up to the porters to fill in the 'blanks on the map' with their local knowledge.

Hansen notes:

That morning I decided to put away my map. With maximum views of about 50 feet beneath the jungle canopy, it wasn't much use. In eight to ten hours of walking each day, we were covering fewer than four miles…since I spent most of my time looking at the ground immediately in front of my feet, I simply followed the best I could. (Hansen, 1988, p.65)

I fell into a similar pattern, following the porters.

> » *How good are the maps you are using to navigate your world?*
>
> » *When was the last time you updated your maps?*

One of the most powerful ways that leaders can serve is by acting as meaning makers and facilitating people in interpreting the landscapes in which they operate. Organizational vision statements and strategic goals, for example, often need to be interpreted before action can be taken. Some of the most common questions people have are: Why? Why now? What does this mean for me? Leaders can share stories from the past that have relevant lessons for the present. Core strengths in the culture can sometimes be applied to current or emerging situations.

What is the role of a leader if they are on totally new terrain, if they do not have the answers, or if they are not clear on which way to go? There are risks in just heading off into the jungle without knowing where you are going. Psychologist Al Sibert suggests that survivors should

…not impose pre-existing patterns on new information but rather allow new information to reshape [their mental models]. The person who has the best chance of handling a situation well is usually the one with the best…mental

Steve Camkin

pictures or images of what is occurring outside his body. (Gonzales, 2004, p.122)

In orienteering and backpacking, the concept of forcing the map to fit the terrain is an example of wishful and overly optimistic thinking. Making the terrain fit our mental model rather than facing the reality upon the ground is an example of imposing pre-existing patterns.

In today's knowledge-based society the way to view leaders is not as being the expert in all things, but as being a facilitator who brings people together to share their maps and expertise. There is wisdom to be gained in sharing different mental models either to create a common understanding or to explore alternative directions. Holding assumptions loosely, asking questions rather than making statements, and searching for alternative interpretations are basic strategies for exploring new pathways. Coutu (2010) in *How Resilience Works* suggests that three core practices can help in finding resilience: facing down reality, searching for meaning, and continually improvising. The searching for meaning Coutu refers to is not "why me?" but rather building bridges from present suffering to a better future. Gonzales (2004) found that survivors spent very little time asking, "why me?" (seeking meaning or taking on a victim role) but rather constructing a more useful meaning and value in the experience (who or what to live for).

One of the things Mukhtar and I were able to do very quickly was to dispassionately face our reality and minimize time and energy spent acting like victims. Holiday (2014), writing in *The Obstacle is the Way* advocates a Stoic philosophical approach of "facing reality and still striving to make something good from it" (p.6). For some reason, I was able to view our situation as an adventure and a challenge. I thought about how I wanted to be during the evolving experience however long it might go on. That vision was a key tool for my self-discipline in spite of the fact that only Mukhtar and I would know the reality of how I had behaved.

Three things I remembered thinking about were: I was not going to complain about the situation; I would never simply "lie down" since "persistence is what makes the impossible possible, the possible likely, and the likely definite" (Robert Half, n.d.); and I would be as creative as I could in thinking and managing our way through our situation. Reflecting back on the experience later I was reminded of George Bernard Shaw's words in *Man vs Superman*: "The reasonable man adapts himself to the world; the unreasonable one persists in trying to adapt the world to himself. Therefore, all progress depends on the unreasonable man." Mukhtar and I also wanted to make progress, but of a different kind.

> » *What challenging situations will you draw lessons from?*

> » *Who might have a different mental map of the situation that you can compare notes with?*

> » *When you look back on this challenging time, how do you want to remember yourself?*

> » *What are you learning now that might help yourself or others in the future?*

To close out this chapter let's circle back to the concept of disorientation and what we can do about those feelings of disorientation by exploring two models from the fields of personal and organizational change.

VUCA. VUCA is a concept that originated with students at the U.S. Army War College. It has become increasingly used in organizations to describe the Volatility, Uncertainty, Complexity, and Ambiguity of today's economic, social, and political environment. For Mukhtar and me, the two strongest aspects of this equation were uncertainty and ambiguity. We were uncertain of the actions of other people; uncertain of where we were; and uncertain as to what we should do and which way to go. The situation was ambiguous because we did not have all the information we needed. There was much complexity. We were trying to balance multiple factors in making the best decisions. While the situation had initially been volatile, it had stabilized once we decided to take no immediate action, but rather to stay in place for a few days.

Ways that organizations can help in VUCA environments include improving access to information; considering whether simple rules to make quick decisions are better than lengthy analyses; promoting systems thinking to understand wider impacts of decisions; and sharing mental models.

SCCC VVRÓ. In seeking to understand personal change, I focus on four main factors that seem to impact how much change people feel they are experiencing: speed, complexity, control, and consequences. Speed refers to the pace at which the change is occurring. With Mukhtar and I, the perception of the speed started slowly with an uneasy feeling that increased as darkness fell on the first day and we found ourselves without porters. That uneasy feeling accelerated when the porters from Apauping did not show up the next morning, reducing the possibility that it was just a delay.

Complexity refers to the number of changes occurring and how much they are inter-related. Suddenly losing a job, for example, may cause changes in finances, relationships, and travel plans. Control refers to how much influence the impacted person feels they have over events. Is the person impacted making the change or is an external event driving the change? Consequences refers to whether the person sees the changes as beneficial or harmful, and how large or small the consequences are for them.

I contend that three main factors can provide a sense of stability for people in the face of turbulent change: vision, values, and relationships. To help reduce the undesired impacts of change, look for ways to help yourself and others reinforce or stabilize around personal vision, values and relationships.

> » *Are there ways you can facilitate connections between people during change, or repair relationships after the change has occurred?*

> » *How can you help minimize adverse consequences to vision, values, or relationships for yourself and others?*

I realized that Mukhtar and my situation did not mean the abandonment of the overall vision, although it might cause delays. I have previously described some of the values I wanted to hold on to, whatever happened. I worked to maintain a good relationship with Mukhtar (at least I hope I did). And I knew that I would be creating concern and inconvenience for others while I was lost, so I tried to reconnect quickly with people at home and in Borneo once we reached Apauping.

> » *What values do you want to model as you go through a challenge?*

> » *Who do you want to build relationships with?*

> » *With whom might you need to repair relationships?*

5

RESOURCES—MAKING THE MOST OF WHAT YOU HAVE

"Tak ada rotan akar pun jadi—
If there are no rattan roots that can be used—
if you can't find the things you need, use something else"

INDONESIAN PROVERB

A survival situation is a ticking clock: You only have so much stored energy…and every time you exert yourself, you're using it up. The trick is to become extremely stingy with your scarce resources, balancing the risk and reward, investing only in efforts that offer the biggest return. (Gonzales, 2004, p.179)

Here is an inventory of the physical items we had in camp, and on ourselves, at the time we realized that things had gone wrong and we would probably have to find our way out of the jungle.

- *Some small deer bones with a little meat left on them*
- *2.5 pounds of rice*
- *½ a small bag of sugar*
- *8 lemon tea sachets*
- *6 spice sachets*
- *20 coffee packets with sugar included*
- *1 large jug of cooking oil*
- *1 small roll of duct tape*
- *1 large blue tarp*
- *1 small orange tarp*
- *1 space blanket*
- *1 hummock*
- *1 lightweight sleeping bag*

Steve Camkin

- *1 sleeping bag liner (silk)*
- *2 pairs of 'Adidas Kampong' rubber shoes*
- *1 pair of lightweight trekking shoes*
- *1 pair of flip flops*
- *1 set of spare shoelaces*
- *Dental floss*
- *2 Toothbrushes*
- *1 tube of toothpaste*
- *1 small roll of toilet paper*
- *1 bug net hat*
- *2 small flashlights*
- *2 backpacks*
- *2 sets of liner socks*
- *3 sets of long football socks*
- *4 long sleeved shirts*
- *3 long pants*
- *1 hat*
- *2 water bottles*
- *40 Malaria tablets*
- *55 Iodine tablets*
- *2 cell phones*
- *1 line of sight radio*
- *Waterproof notebook*

- *Pen*

- *Pencil*

- *Pocket book of survival tips*

- *Signal mirror*

- *Whistle (less psychologically stressful to use than yelling, but also somewhat less effective because birds mimic the sound)*

- *Machete with a number of nicks in it*

- *1 small pocket-knife*

- *1 small bottle of insect repellent*

- *2 pairs of reading glasses*

- *1 box of matches*

- *1 flint striker*

- *1 disposable cigarette lighter*

- *8 plastic bags of different sizes*

- *1 first aid kit*

- *1 tube of Chapstick*

- *1 tube of antibiotic cream*

- *1 watch*

It is not what is in your backpack that gets you through; it is what is in your head and heart that gets you through.

When you realize you are lost, or in a precarious situation, one of the first steps Search and Rescue specialists recommend after managing any immediate threats, is to take an inventory of what you have. After you have taken the inventory, think about other ways you could use your resources other than for the obvious. Is a tarp just a rain cover, or could it be used for gathering water, a sleeping layer, or a signaling device? Many survival stories tell of people discarding items along the way in their rush to get back to 'civilization'. Searchers are often puzzled that many of the discarded items could have been helpful in other ways. Sometimes it is desperation as people run out of energy; sometimes people do not realize what they have with them. Similar principles apply in life and in business when there is a major change or any unanticipated event.

» *What are some of your current resources? Now, envision various creative uses for your resources.*

Because so much of our identity is often tied up with our work, we tend to focus on financial and physical resources and neglect other resources we have available to us. When projects fall behind at work, the refrain is often that we need more people, more time, or more money. Resources come in many forms- including physical, mental, emotional, relational, spiritual, financial, time, and information.

Resources vs. Resourcefulness. A key lesson I re-learned during this most recent time in the Borneo jungle was connected to resource assessment, management, and usage. Most families and organizations do not have unlimited resources and we sometimes underestimate our resourcefulness. There is a difference between resources and resourcefulness. Resources are the items in your pack; resourcefulness is how you use them, how you find new uses for what you have, or how you find other resources in the environment around you. During my trip I was struck by the contrast in the manufactured items I brought along and the items that villagers were able to adapt, on the spot, from local materials.

There is an Australian Aboriginal saying that "the more you know the less you need". For nicks and cuts, for example, I could use my own antibiotic cream or, if we could find the sakali-olo leaf, it could be chewed to a paste and smeared on the skin to stop bleeding and prevent infection (Hansen, 1988, p.69).

When one experiences a crisis, the focus is often on what is lost or will be lost. Deficit thinking sets in exacerbating stress and robbing our ability to use the mental, physical, emotional, and spiritual resources we do have.

> » *In what areas of your life have you allowed deficit thinking to creep in and limit your thinking about options and resources?*

Types of energy as resources. Energy is a resource, as is time. Although I cannot find the original source anymore, I was struck years ago by the findings of research conducted at the Australian Institute of Sport. Athletes that had the longest and most successful careers appeared to manage and balance four types of energy: mental, emotional, physical, and relational. Mental energy is about focus. Emotional energy is about the qualities a person brings to a situation. Physical energy relates to what the body brings. Relational energy relates to the synergies that relationships bring. Conflict in relationships can also impact individual emotional energy and contributes to loss of energy in individuals, teams, or organizations. Mental and emotional energies are used for initiating activity; physical and relational energies are used for sustaining activity over time.

I would add two other types of energy—spiritual and financial. Spiritual energy has to do with meaning and purpose. It is both an initiating and sustaining energy. Financial energy ($, cash flow) is an enabler for change. Many projects cannot be not sustained if funding is not maintained.

> » *What are you better at initiating/starting activities and projects, or sustaining those activities and projects?*
>
> » *What is your organization better at?*

Schwartz and McCarthy (2007) argue that managing energy is more important to productivity than the traditional approach of managing time. In the situation Mukhtar and I were in, we needed to balance both time and energy. Neither was an unlimited resource. Mukhtar and I certainly did not have much food for physical energy, especially considering the demands if we needed to trek by ourselves across the country for an undetermined period of time. Mukhtar and I did have some other kinds of resources or energy—financial, relational, spiritual, emotional, and mental.

Financial. We had some cash with us, but that was useless while we were on our own in the deep jungle. The paper money could be used for lighting fires, first aid, or for writing on.

Relational. Since we were out of contact with the rest of the world, we would need just to rely on each other and could not draw directly on other people. Mukhtar had brief connections with the porters in Long Layu and Apauping. We both had people outside the area and at home who were expecting us to report back, however, they were not expecting us to report for quite a few days.

Mukhtar and I knew we were much stronger together than apart. One African proverb says "If you want to go fast, go alone. If you want to go far, go together". Another African proverb says that "When spiders unite, they can tie down a lion." Together we would share tasks, watch out for each other, balance each other's energy, and observe more of the terrain. To make the most of that synergy we would also need to manage the energy of the relationship.

Mukhtar has led treks into some of the most challenging regions of Sulawesi, Kalimantan, and Papua with clients of varying ability levels; he brought them through powerful experiences unscathed. These are regions that still pose substantial challenges for travel due to remoteness, communication difficulties, tough terrain, flooded rivers, and impassible roads. After Mukhtar and I emerged from the jungle, I asked him what helped him through our and his other challenging jungle experiences. He commented: "What helps me get through tough times is when clients don't feel panicked and angry and want to be invited to discussions to find solutions" (Makussara, 2020). We often think of resilience from an individual perspective. Mukhtar's wise comments reminded me that resilience often occurs in a social context. We impact each other by our responses to stress and how we demonstrate calmness, creative thinking, and resilience.

I have found the concept of an 'emotional bank account' popularized by Covey (1989) useful, especially the notion of making deposits before you need actually them. I was sure that at multiple points I would be leaning heavily on Mukhtar's physical strength and expertise, however, I wanted to minimize that reliance as much as I could. I wanted to be an equal partner as much as I could. I tried to find ways to 'deposit' early and often to our emotional bank account. I could have taken a role just as a client on the trek, however, that is not my style, nor would it have been helpful to us succeeding in this situation. I took on the tasks of collecting firewood and water while Mukhtar was setting up the rest of camp; I did some scouting for resources at the different locations. Sometimes I led the way when our immediate direction was apparent.

Trust. The basis of a strong relationship is interpersonal trust. Research over several years has identified some key components needed to establish, build, and maintain trust. Aspects of making and keeping agreements (contractual trust), mutual open sharing (self-disclosure trust), and establishing a safe environment (physical trust) are key to strong relationships.

Contractual trust involves the "confident anticipation that people will do what they say they will do" (Mink, Owen & Mink, 1993, p.83). This is important because "people need predictability and order in their lives" (Mink, Owen & Mink, 1993, p.83). Self-disclosure trust is the willingness to engage in reciprocal openness and sharing, because "if someone withholds information from you, you may feel manipulated, controlled, or deceived" (Mink, Owen & Mink, 1993, p.83). Physical trust is a feeling that the "… physical and psychological environment is safe" (Mink, Owen &

Mink, 1993, p.83). Intentions and competence, the desire and the ability of the other person to do the right thing by you, are "two threads [that] tie these three aspects of trust together" (Mink, Owen &Mink, 1993, p.83).

CCR. In my own reflection on trust, I have considered three main factors—character, competence, and relationship. Do I believe this person is a good person? Can and will they do what they say they will do? Do I trust that our goals are aligned? During my time in the jungle, the acronym CCR came to mind a number of times because I associated the letters with Creedence Clearwater Revival's song about the rain in the jungle of Vietnam. It reminded me of both the situation Mukhtar and I were in and the need to continue to build and maintain trust between us.

It was the stories Mukhtar related and what he shared about himself that laid the foundation for me to trust him. My trust only deepened as I observed him in many circumstances. In Mukhtar, I saw very early someone with a depth of character, an incredible work ethic, profound caring for his family, and who was striving to provide me with an exceptional experience in the jungle that he loved so much. His competence in the jungle was quickly evident in the way he moved, accomplished tasks, and how he demonstrated deep knowledge about the jungle and the local people. Our relationship was further solidified from what I sensed were our similar goals and values, and from his candor when he shared stories including past challenges with other trekkers. For two people who had only recently met, spoke different languages, and grew up very differently, I felt that Mukhtar and I built a strong, supportive, and trusting relationship quickly.

> » *Who do you have strong relationships with?*

> » *What aspects of trust are present in those relationships?*

> » *With whom do you need to improve a relationship?*

» *Where would you start? Would you start by having them understand your character; being aware of your competence; or by strengthening the relationship?*

Positive Intent. Every relationship has test points. There were a few of these test points early in this trip. It would have been very easy for Mukhtar or me to resort to unproductive blaming of each other, the porters, unclear maps, etc. I generally find assuming positive intent on the part of others very helpful. Since I am a non-Indonesian speaker and a cultural outsider, I tried to assume no negative intent. I also knew that coming on this adventure was not going to be like signing up for a heavily scheduled package tour. I expected that adaptations would need to be made and that things were likely to go wrong at times. However, I was confident Mukhtar, and I would be able to work together, adapt, and overcome.

Spiritual Energy. Mukhtar has massive reserves of strength and resilience. His knowledge and expertise were gained through life experiences rather than from reading books on the topic. When I asked Mukhtar, what has built resilience in his life he said: "The thing that has built resilience in my life is that I always pray and try to finish with a simple pattern and do not forget to exercise every day".

"As Peter Leschak comments, "Whether a deity is actually listening, or not, there is value in formally announcing your needs, desires, worries, sins and goals in a focused, prayerful attitude. Only when you are aware, can you take action. Survival psychologists have observed the same thing" (Gonzales, p.180). "Survival psychologists have long observed that successful survivors pray, even when they don't believe in a god" (Gonzales, 2004, p. 204). Researchers (Alim *et al*, 2008; Min *et al*, 2012; Gonzales, 2004; Sherwood, 2009) have pointed to the importance in survival situations of spirituality, a sense of purpose, or other reasons to live. During the time I was in the Australian Army, I had often been told that "there are no atheists in foxholes". Spiritual texts have recognized the interrelated dilemmas of being lost and the emotional and physical fatigue that often follows: "And He found you lost and guided [you]. And He found you poor and made [you] self-sufficient" (Quran 93:7-8). "But those who hope in the Lord will renew their strength. They will soar on wings like eagles; they will run and not grow weary, they will walk and not be faint" (Isaiah 40:31). We will explore additional aspects of spiritual energy later in our story.

Emotional Energy. Emotional energy refers to the emotional quality that we bring to tasks or situations, the feelings associated with that energy, and whether that energy is helpful or unhelpful at any point in time.

Emotional and physical energies are closely interconnected. Unhelpful energy, like debilitating anxiety or misplaced anger, can drain us of physical energy or at least divert that energy from where it can be more helpfully directed. The assertion that "fatigue makes cowards of us all" has been attributed to both General Patton and to the American football coach Vince Lombardi. While energy management is relevant to all of us, it is an especially important competency for leaders. A quote attributed to Noel Tichy, an American management consultant states:

> Simply put, a leader's job is to energize others. Notice that I don't say it's part of the job; it is their job. There is no 'time off' when a leader isn't responsible for energizing others. Every interaction a leader has is either going to positively energize those around them or negatively energize them.

Emotional intelligence, or the skillful use of emotions, has been linked by researchers to resilience through the increased ability to view events as challenges rather than threats and, therefore, manage potential impacts of stress more effectively (Schneider, Lyons & Khazon, 2013; Sarrionandia, Ramos-Diaz & Fernandez-Lasarte, 2018). Emotional energy is also closely connected to relational energy through the mechanism of Emotional Intelligence. Emotional Intelligence is compromised of four skills – self-awareness; self-management; social awareness and relationship management (Bradberry & Greaves, 2009). Two of these skills (self-awareness and self-management) support personal competence by managing emotions by either avoiding loss of energy through unhelpful, negative emotions, or by building energy through positive, helpful emotions. Two of these skills (social awareness, [understanding our impacts on others]; and relationship management) help prevent loss of energy through unhelpful conflict and tension. Change often damages relationships so anything we can do to effectively manage ourselves and our relationships during stressful times helps builds our resilience.

Emotional energy and storytelling. Organizations are increasingly utilizing the power of storytelling as a way to emotionally and positively engage workers, customers, or key stakeholders. Storytelling also has value in building resilience.

> People can cultivate positive emotions by learning to change the stories they tell themselves about the events in their lives. Often, people …cast themselves in the role of victim, blaming others or external circumstances for their problems. Becoming aware of the difference between the facts in a given situation and the way we interpret those facts can be powerful in itself. … [we] have a choice about how to view a given event and to recognize how powerfully the story [we] tell influences the emotions [we] feel. (Schwartz and McCarthy, 2007 p.71).

> » *How can we tell ourselves the "most hopeful and personally empowering story possible in any given situation, without denying or minimizing the facts" (Schwartz & McCarthy, 2007, p.71).*

Mukhtar and I met many great storytellers in our time together in Borneo. In this region, stories have served many purposes for centuries beyond mere entertainment. Stories are and have been a way to transmit knowledge down the generations, and across wandering tribes about where to find food and other resources (Puri, 2005, p.267). Stories are also a way of creating mental maps of the terrain.

Mukhtar told many stories about us for entertainment and to build relationships and goodwill. Some of those stories he re-told multiple times. I could not understand the details of the stories that Mukhtar related in Indonesian. However, judging from the impact he had on his listeners, Mukhtar is a very skilled storyteller. He often used humor to relieve tension and to bring people over to our side. He related how he was following the 'orang gila puti' (the crazy white man). He made the complicated story of our overall journey (traveling North to South across Borneo using only human power) simple through the repetition of key phrases. He built my credibility with the locals by sharing stories of my being willing to try any food and how I managed our epic 12-hour mud-slog from Long Bawan to Long Layu.

> » *What parts of your life story do you remember and re-tell?*
>
> » *What are the lessons you have learned from these stories?*
>
> » *What collection of stories do you have that you share that captures who you are, and what you value?*

Celebrating small wins. Celebrating small wins is one way to maintain emotional energy. Gonzales writes "survivors find wealth and happiness in the smallest things" (Gonzales, 2004, p.223). He quotes Callahan who spent 38 days adrift: "My plight has given me a strange kind of wealth. I value each moment that is not spent in pain, desperation, hunger or thirst" (Gonzales, 2004, p.225). I recognized that the occasional food items that Mukhtar and I found like Umbud root or the fern tip soup that Mukhtar made did not add much in the way of calories, however, they were our small wins. These foods brought a small sense of celebration and variety to routine days of slogging through mud and pushing ourselves uphill or wading down rivers. Another form of small wins or celebrations lay in the natural experiences we encountered including clear, cascading waterfalls, colorful fungi, soaring hornbills, or a particularly lush section of creekline.

Mental Energy. Mental energy helps us focus on the important things; mental toughness helps us to maintain that focus in the face of distractions. Both Mukhtar and I have major strengths in this area. I assessed from the stories Mukhtar told me about his childhood and some of his earlier expeditions, that he was a very mentally tough person. I have been tested on other long expeditions around the globe, in the Australian and New Zealand Armies, and with Outward Bound.

Mukhtar has a deep knowledge of jungle regions even though he had only been in this general area about five years back. I have outdoor experiences as well as transferable skills from my work as a leadership and team development specialist including knowledge of how the brain operates under stress when making decisions. From my studies in Neuroscience and Neurolinguistic Programming (NLP), I understand something of bias in decision-making and the importance of managing mental frames. There is a strong connection between physical, emotional, and mental states; we can impact one state by conscious attempts to impact the others. I knew Mukhtar and I would need to manage all these to be successful.

Specific information on trails, roads, and villages was the resource we lacked. As noted previously, there are no meaningful maps of the area. The maps that do exist are of a totally inadequate scale for navigation, are often outdated, show villages or roads that no longer exist, or do not show forestry roads that do exist. Information is locked up in the heads of local experts and we no longer had access to them. Knowledge of the jungle trails in Borneo is rapidly being lost as people no longer rely on those trails, but use roads, air, or mechanized boats. Unfortunately, Mukhtar and I were now getting an appreciation of the impact of the loss of local knowledge. We had encountered challenges finding and hiring local Lundeyah guides back in Long Layu. Our decision to 'meet in the jungle' had been at least partly based on an assumption about the depth and current of knowledge of local guides. While their fathers and grandfathers had regularly traveled the trail from Long Layu to Apauping, younger villagers had not, and the transmission of local knowledge was fast eroding. Even the notion of portering was shifting as a result of improved or changed road, river, and air access.

Mental Energy. Watch your language. I think I only swore a couple of times, and that was to myself. It is part of my nature not to swear; I also saw it as an exercise in self-discipline. Emotions connected with swearing, for me at least, are tied to a temporary loss of control, focus, and discipline.

Another way to watch your language is to notice the metaphors that you use to explain the world around you. I could choose to view the experience as a 'battle', or a 'mistake', or I could choose to view it as a personal challenge and adventure. Metaphors are a key part of the stories we create for ourselves.

> » *What metaphors are you using to describe situations?*

> » *How are those metaphors impacting the way you see and act in the world?*

> » *How is your language impacting how you see and deal with a situation?*

Mental Energy and Framing—Wants vs. Needs. Re-framing is a powerful tool to use during challenging circumstances. One frame is wants vs. needs; one of the issues contributing to deficit thinking is the inability to distinguish between those wants and needs. The body, for example, can go weeks without food, but only a few days without water. Mukhtar and I were able to find plenty of water with the exception of one night where we slept high on a ridge. We were often hungry, but we both knew that food was more in the want category than in the need category, at least for quite a few days. The Masai have a saying: "Do not allow the belly to make you useless".

I enjoy sleeping on a mattress back home. Most people in Kalimantan sleep on a mat on the floor so while in Borneo I had been sleeping on a floor mat for a while. Initially, I found it uncomfortable, however, once I got used to it, I found that sleeping on a floor mat helped any issues I had with back pain and tightness.

Changing expectations preemptively or facing reality is a technique that I have often found helpful. Instead of wanting to be out of the situation, I focused on what I could control given the situation. I did not complain that there was no mattress to sleep on, instead, I chose to look for a dry place to place my mat to sleep. I would not expect a smoke-free tent, instead, I would appreciate and adjust to a tent where there was just enough smoke to keep insects away while not being unbearable. I would not expect a full meal; instead, I would appreciate the taste of some fern-tip and spice soup.

We all have cultural frames around food. I have eaten snake before. In Borneo Python is not just an emergency food, it is a delicacy and brings high prices. Similarly, Bird's Nest Soup is a Chinese delicacy and harvested widely in Kalimantan. It is basically hardened saliva from Swiftlet nests, and it is rich in iron, calcium, magnesium, and potassium. Mukhtar shared some stories of the Tiong O'Hang area. In the years between 1980-2000 *Belatu Cave produced 6600 pounds per year of Swallow nests @ over 375,000 IR [$10.90 USD per pound]. Murders were committed over Swallow nests. Ownership rights for caves were strongly defended. People slept in the caves a month at a time to protect the harvests. Nests from natural caves produce better quality soup however. Prices are lower now because of artificial nests in buildings that have been created to attract Swallows.*

> » *What are you treating as a need that is actually a want?*

> » *What wants are getting in the way of you meeting your needs?*

Mental Energy and Creative Thinking. As mentioned previously, one way to expand creative thinking and the use of resources is to think not merely about what the item is, but also what qualities the item has and how those qualities could help you see other uses for the item. Dental floss, for example, can be used as a shoelace, repair thread, or for medical stitches. Plastic bags can be used as a float, a raincoat, a water carrier, or a barrier for a punctured lung. Later in the trip when we ran out of insect repellent and sunscreen, we used mud as a shield from the intense sun and from the insects.

Here are just a few ways that the Dyak use bamboo: young shoots for food; a water or food storage device; firewood; a marker to point the way on a trail; a frame for rice sacks for a bed; materials to create a fish trap; and a spear or a fishhook. A piece of bamboo split lengthways and then sideways formed a cup-holder at one abandoned camp Mukhtar and I passed.

> *Look around your environment and pick one item. How many different uses can you think of for that item apart from its normal use?*

As I am writing this book, the COVID-19 pandemic is rolling through cities, regions, and countries. People are challenged to find new ways to work and to connect with others. Businesses are scrambling to find creative ways to deliver products and services and are looking for opportunities for new products and services. In-room dining establishments are now doing drive-by delivery, educational institutions are rapidly converting from face-to-face learning to virtual delivery of learning, and one young Australian entrepreneur who is a wedding planner developed a booming (and now international) business of conducting drive-by weddings. Good on ya, Melissa! A ski resort in Colorado has converted Gondola cars into small dining spaces for small 'bubbles' of people. The Gondolas come equipped with dining benches, Bluetooth connections for music and a light to signal for service.

> *What new ways can you think of to deliver or present your products and services to a current market, or to create a new market?*

'Survival' shows on television often highlight traditional fire-lighting skills. Mukhtar and I had plenty of matches with us and a disposable lighter. However, the wood we encountered was often quite wet, so our main challenge was getting the wood to catch after we had struck the match. Over time I learned to find certain types of wood that ignited more easily than others. Mukhtar and I found many ways to create fire accelerants using materials we had at hand. Small pieces of rubber, strips of plastic, waxed notebook covers, and even insect repellent served as fire accelerants.

One technique used by the Dyak and Penan for lighting fires is to create "fire curls". Sticks about ½" across are shaved back in curls to expose the dryer inner wood. It is amazing how quickly the locals can create a bundle of fire curl sticks. For me, unpracticed in this skill, it took some time.

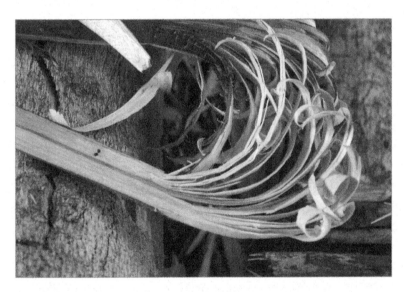

Tree sap (Damar resin) that looks like chunks of rock is another resource the locals use. After Mukhtar showed me what to look for, I became quite good at finding these chunks of sap. We carried chunks with us from camp to camp. There used to be quite a local resin industry from World War II until the 1960's collecting and trading Damar resin, but that industry has collapsed now (Puri,

2005, p. 57) and has largely been replaced by disposable lighters, gasoline, and other similar items.

Hansen describes how the Penan made fire using batu api (fire-rock or flint) before the introduction of matches or disposable lighters.

> Holding the flint and a thin mat of tinder between his thumb and first two finger-tips, Bo'Hok vigorously struck the smooth surface of the [green length of] bamboo at an oblique angle. To my astonishment sparks appeared. The tinder soon glowed red in patches and was then placed into a prepared handful of dried fibrous sago barked mixed with ash from burned leaves...Bo 'Hok added wood shavings, blew two or three times and with seconds we had fire. (Hansen, 1988, p.141)

There is also a vine called akar kopek or 'matches vine'. Once lit, the dried vine smolders for days and is a convenient way to transport fire (Hansen, 1988, p.157).

> » *What are the ways you have found to accelerate the adoption of an idea, or the use of a new product or service?*

I noticed that the locals had a different way of tending fires than the way I was taught. I was taught to gradually build the size of the fire by layering increasingly large sticks and paying constant attention to blowing and fanning. I noticed this was less effective sometimes than the Borneo style of bundling things together and leaving it alone to catch and spread. I wondered if it could be that we can smother fires, new ideas, and people with too much attention?

> » *What kinds of energy (physical, emotional, mental, relational, spiritual, financial) do you have the most of at the moment?*

> » *What kind of energy do you have the least of?*

> » *What kinds of energy does your organization have the most of at the moment?*

> » *What kinds of energy does your organization have the least of now?*

> » *What can you do to find or build up the kinds of energy you or your organization needs?*

Time vs. Energy Management. As mentioned previously, Schwartz and McCarthy (2007) argue that it is more effective to manage our energy than our time. While they write about business contexts, it was also a very helpful lens to use in thinking through situations like the one Mukhtar and I found ourselves in. While we needed to balance energy and time, energy management was more important than time management. We were more likely to make critical mistakes if our physical energy was too low or if our concentration drifted. Time is a resource; so is energy. For some organizations in certain stages of their life cycle speed is essential. For other organizations, smart and efficient use of other resources is more important.

When I first started work in Australia, part of the cultural tradition in some organizations was morning and afternoon tea. In Government agencies, there was usually a 'Tea Lady' that brought tea, cookies, and cake around on a trolley to the various work areas. In 2020, as part of company efforts at building resilience, Google launched a check-in process they termed TEA (Thoughts, Energy, Attention).

> Where are your thoughts? Where is your energy? Where is your attention? And as we look at those three…Is it time to take on a new challenging project? Is your energy low? Do you need to jump up and down? Do you need to step away? Do you need to take a nap? And where is your attention? What is the one thing you can focus on today that you can control, that you can influence, that will give you purpose and meaning and optimism for today? (Vasel, 2020)

>> *How often do you check in with yourself on your thoughts, your energy, and your attention?*

>> *How often do you check in with others?*

>> *What are the most important resources you or your organization needs to manage while going through changes?*

Too many resources. Sometimes you can have too much of a good thing. Once the porters left, Mukhtar and I decided that we should 'self-rescue' if no one showed up in a few days. One of the challenges we had was deciding what to take with us.

Mukhtar and I had only two small packs. We knew that carrying heavy packs would: slow us down and also increase the risk of injury; tire us out more easily; cause us to burn more calories. Mukhtar and I talked and decided what was essential, and what might actually be a burden. This was our own 'Lost in the Jungle' priority exercise similar to one that has been a popular team decision-making exercise.

Later, various newspapers that commented on our experience reported that we were ill-equipped, however, I did not feel that way with the exception of the lack of food. We had shelter, fire lighting equipment, appropriate clothes and there were many resources that we drew upon in the jungle.

Mukhtar and I left behind the large blue tarp that had been our sleeping shelter and took a smaller one which was much lighter. We left behind most of a large container of cooking oil as it was just too heavy, but we took the remainder of the food and the drink sachets.

> » *Are you burdening yourself or other people by hanging onto "stuff" you should let go of (material possessions, expectations, negative feelings, etc.)?*
>
> » *If you are making a change in your personal or professional life, what do you need to leave behind?*
>
> » *What are you holding onto that is not likely to be helpful to you in the future?*

6

ROLLING THE DICE

"Know when to hold 'em, know when to fold 'em"

THE GAMBLER

DECEMBER 20TH, 2019
Durian Tree Camp (Night 2)

Woke up just after dawn. Cool night but I was snug. Rain drizzled overnight and also at 8am. There doesn't seem to be a real pattern to the rainfall except that the heaviest rain falls in the late afternoon. My back is tight, perhaps too much bend in the hummock? No sign of porters by 7am. Our immediate plan is to sit tight for the day as the porters can move more easily than us and know the area better. We will conserve our minimal food (tea and sugar for breakfast; rice soup for lunch). My minor throat infection seems to have gotten worse overnight. Lots of coughing.

Mukhtar has had a lot of experience dealing with hunger and knows how to make do with limited resources. He was the youngest of 7 children raised by a single mother. I have been on Australian and New Zealand Army survival exercises and an Outward Bound three-day 'solo' experience where we were given minimal rations; I know a little of the psychological impacts of hunger and of how long the body can go without food. Hunger will not be our biggest challenge. *Mukhtar is originally from Makassar, Sulawesi where they grow corn and potatoes. They fish a lot. Our short rations reminded him of growing up in Sulawesi. Sometimes only one meal per day. He used to go into the jungle at 13 years old to find wood and barter it for food. Meals were often corn and fish. Sometimes the base of a banana tree sliced very thin. In those days rice was only eaten by the richer people such as teachers and government employees.*

One day he went without food for 3 days. He was on his own in the jungle and very weak when three people came by and rescued him. He thinks those three people saved his life. His mother didn't know where he had gone and his father had separated from his mother. His mother had no education. He was very sad for his mother who worked very hard.

One of the stories Mukhtar told me was how he would help prepare sago since it was one starch they could find for food. "Sago palm is known to be poisonous and sago separation includes careful processes to remove these toxins, before they are edible. Intake of sago before proper processing to remove toxins can cause vomiting, liver damage, and even death" (Lal, 2003).

Mukhtar became a guide in an unusual way. He was washing buses in Samarinda, a big coastal town in Eastern Kalimantan when a couple connected with him and asked him to show them around. They gave him a big tip at the end of the day. A similar thing happened soon after. He got curious soon after these experiences. He bought a new shirt, long pants and a book on the English language and went about teaching himself English. He served as a guide for just tips for a year while he learned English. He later met Lucas, who was working at a hotel and now runs the company that contracted Mukhtar for our trip.

Mukhtar tries walking downriver a bit to try calling out again to anyone that might be in the area. *We are both still trying to figure out what is going on with the incoming porters. Worst* case seems to be that we are both waiting in different "old village" sites and then the Apauping porters turn back. The decision of whether to stay where we were or to make our own way out of the jungle was not a simple one to make. There were risks both to staying and to going. The situation was ambiguous. There was no clean mathematical formula.

> » *How do you make decisions when the data is 'split' or when you don't have enough information?*

> » *How does continuous decision-making in an ambiguous environment impact your energy?*

For us to go alone would probably take three days with route finding and big packs-compared to two with the porters. We also have little food. We would leave behind the big blue tarp. We are starting to calculate what is non-essential if we need to travel on our own. I remember the story of Scott of the Antarctic's precious rock samples that they dragged across Antarctica as they were dying of malnutrition. What to take, what to leave? Our food stocks are 2.5 pounds of rice, ½ a bag of sugar and some tea, coffee and lemon tea packets. We are going to keep most of that for travel.

Heard Gibbons close by. M comes back from another reconnoiter to see if he can find the trail and now thinks we may be at an old Gaharu wood collectors camp rather than an old village. We walked 1.5 hours from the last camp to here. Mukhtar's latest foray confirms that we are in a valley with layers of hills on each side. The valley curves around. It is a poor position for a line-of-sight radio or even smoke. M thinks the porters have made a mistake in the drop-off location. I consider the possibility that there was miscommunication in defining the rendezvous point.

We have started taking inventory of the resources we have and how we can improvise. I was re-reading my emergency first aid book and it mentions the pages are waxed for fire starting. The staples for the pages can be used for fishhooks (very small I think) and the center Mylar pages could be used for signaling (if we had any sun and were in an open space). Insect repellent works as a fire starter. I am carrying a flint starter. We have floss that can be used for stitching or fishing line; the batteries in the camera might be potential fire starters. Plastic bags can be used for a raincoat.

Looks like more deer soup for dinner tonight although we have really scraped all the meat off the bones already so it's more likely to be "meat flavored" soup. M chops up the bones, presumably to get to the marrow. His machete has developed some deep nicks, probably from wood chopping. (Later we will joke that as a self-defense tool against animals it would work better if we just throw the machete.)

Much of the wood in the forest is wet to some degree. We have a platform over the fire that acts as a drying rack for wood that will be used later. It also works well for drying socks, shirts etc. I shaved today to kill time and because it was getting itchy.

I took a wash in the stream at 2pm and we started a fire for tea, which took three hours to boil! M went scouting up the hill and found a potential trail to Apauping. He also brought back some wood which he quickly split using the machete. He couldn't find kaya ohang wood which lights very easily even in the wet season. When I asked how to spot it he said it is a small tree with a diameter of about 3" Helpful! Two small trees are enough for two days camping but the tree is not common. M says everyone looks for it especially in the wet season. The rain is back at 2:45 pm. The most common birds we have been hearing are woodpeckers and flycatchers. There are some small brown butterflies and a couple of larger ones like swallowtails. M said he saw monkey, hornbills, gibbons and a civet on his scouting trip this morning. The smoke from the fire has been shifting direction today. Could this indicate a shift in weather patterns?"

Steve Camkin

Heavy rain at 4:40 p.m. with wind. M is slogging away at the fire, fanning and blowing to make our deer-flavored soup. I keep offering to do more and feel lazy, but I also don't want to mess up the guide/client relationship. If the roles were reversed, I know I would be doing the same. Doing my best to conserve heat and energy staying dry in my hummock. Thin deer soup for dinner, more gristle and less meat each time we reuse the bones.

DECEMBER 21ST, 2019
Durian Tree Camp (Night 3)

Tried using the space blanket wrapped around me as a cocoon last night. It worked fairly well for warmth, but it doesn't let the moisture out. I was warm until near dawn. Crawled out of my cocoon just after 6am.

Decision today about whether to stay or go. I think today is December 23rd. Date was recorded incorrectly. *If we go back to Long Layu I think we will get there by the afternoon of the 24th. We would spend Christmas in Long Layu and then either a) Hike Long Layu to Apauping by foot b) Hike just the section of trail we missed near Long Layu then go back to Long Layu. From there we could take a 4WD back to Long Bawan, fly to Tanjung Selor. Take a boat upriver from there to Apauping. Hike from Apauping to our current site and back to Apauping.* An inelegant solution to getting the overall expedition back on track but it would do the trick. *From Apauping we would continue our journey rafting down to Punjungan, on the Sungai Punjungan and then hiking up to Jelet. Looking further forward the section between Jelet and Data Dian sounds remote, interesting and possibly again tricky for logistics.*

We explored the pros and cons further of various options: staying where we were; returning to Long Layu; or trying to find our way to Apauping.

Pros for staying

- *Easier for others to move and track to us*
- *Less risk of missing the porters if everyone is moving*
- *Less risk of getting lost*
- *Less risk of an injury*
- *Conserve energy*

Cons for staying

- *We are in a poor location to be found easily*
- *We are not sure the Long Layu porters are clear on our location*
- *Help might take some time to get to us*
- *The porters in Apauping do not currently know our situation*
- *Possibility that the two groups of porters might not communicate*

Unknowns for staying

- *When will the Apauping porters realize we have not arrived at the original meeting point?*
- *Will the porters be willing to look for us again?*
- *What is the risk of triggering a full search?*

Pros for Traveling to Apauping (This route should pass a large grassy area with lots of wild deer and wild buffalo).

- *Direction is simple* later proven untrue!

- *Roughly in line with expected direction of Apauping porters*

- *Helps us stay on program for the larger expedition*

- *Might shorten the time to connect with porters from Apauping*

- *M traveled in the area 5 years ago*

Cons for traveling to Apauping

- *Don't know the trail across country*

- *We might pass the porters on the way*

- *Heavy packs*

- *If porters come back from Long Layu, it increases the risk they will not find us; or the time needed to catch up with us*

- *Lose a comfortable camp where we can stay dry and conserve energy*

Pros for traveling to Long Layu

- *Have a marked trail; more of a known*

- *Might catch a ride in a boat on the last section into Long Layu*

- *1-2 days (M thinks we could do it in 1 day; I think that is optimistic)*

- *Might intercept the Long Layu porters if they come back to look for us*

- *From Long Layu we can re-start the expedition after getting to Apauping*

Cons for traveling to Long Layu

- *Might miss the Apauping porters*
- *Have to climb back over the mountain and navigate two river systems*
- *Lost days since we have not gotten to Apauping*
- *Might miss the Long Layu porters*

M has gone out again to look for Umbud for soup. Waiting at the camp gives me more time to get to know Mukhtar. He has an apartment he rents in Samarinda because most of his work is in Borneo. His family lives in Sulawesi and he visits them 2-3 times a year. This allows him to send money back home to his family. He has 5 kids aged 12-22. Three boys not married, two girls. The youngest boy is apparently very good at Math and wants to do coding.

We decide to wait one more day diary error? *and will get up early, head back towards Long Layu, and try to get back to our start point on day one. We will then follow the river on the other side where there is supposed to be a trail back to Long Layu. Not sure that the Apauping porters can locate us where we are. Not sure the Long Layu porters know they have dropped us in the wrong location. Not sure when and how the Long Layu porters will contact the Apauping porters -or if they will contact them if they believe they have dropped us in the correct location. Returning to Long Layu seems the quicker and less risky alternative.*

Most people in survival situations push on rather than back-track (Sherwood, 2009). Koester (2008), after examining lost person behavior across many years and many cases, developed a series

Steve Camkin

of profiles of 'lost person' behaviors that are used world-wide by Search and Rescue organizations.

DECEMBER 21ST, 2019
Durian Tree Camp

Saw some blue sky this morning for 45 minutes. Light rain at 11:15 am. Got some good photos of light "star bursting" through trees and smoke from the campfire.

The light playing off ferns by the creek and the towering trees was mesmerizing after days of gloom. At one point the light shone through like a Christian cross and for some reason, it provided a sense of security for me.

In retrospect, instead of taking photos, I should have used my watch and the sun to try to get a directional fix as we saw little or no sun over the next week. Perhaps I was still thinking the porters would arrive; perhaps I was under-reacting to our situation.

I hear the tok, tok, tok of woodpeckers. We have had three deadfalls (falling tree branches) *on the trip so far come down close to us. Rain at 2:50 pm. Took an afternoon nap. M tells me the story of a Dutch tourist. They were trekking near Puruk Cahu. Mukhtar was 26 and the tourist was 21. M says their next section should take two days. The tourist says it should be one; he doesn't want to take shelter, food; etc. He doesn't eat enough breakfast, so M wraps some rice in leaves. The tourist gets very, very tired but suddenly some seekers of Gaharu wood invited them into their camp for coffee, rice and meat—but the tourist only has coffee. The tourist wants to keep going in the rain at 7pm. They pushed on. Three steps forward, 2 back on the uphill. M gets very tired also. Both fainted. Employees of a logging company found them, gave them food and took them by jeep to the river.*

I pushed Mukhtar to tell me more stories.

Tourist story 2: Two young 25-year-old trekkers found a sandy bank on the river to rest on while M is cooking lunch. M hears thunder and warns them about the danger of a flash flood. M keeps cooking but calls them to lunch warning them of the risk of a flash flood. The trekkers leave the sandbank and shortly after lunch a flash flood roars by.

Tourist story 3: Another time his German clients say they will not pay him the guide fee unless he climbs to the top of a mountain where the birds' nests are. This involves exposed rock climbing and multiple sections of climbing up rattan vines. Mukhtar says he has a strong fear of heights when there are not trees below him and the clients wanted him to go first. M says he cried going up and down (I'm not sure if he means literally.) He says he climbed back down hand over hand, sometimes closing and then reopening his eyes for brief periods. Later at the end of the trip, when I asked Mukhtar about his impressions of me, he said: "I appreciated that you did not treat me as a slave". I was struck by the strength and emotion in that statement. Reflecting on some of his past experiences, I started to understand why. I had been hoping to have more of a partner relationship on such a long trip, rather than a Guide/Client relationship.

Thunder rolls in. A handful of rice and tea with sugar for dinner tonight! Heavy rain overnight but stopped by the morning.

DECEMBER 22ND, 2019
From Durian Tree Camp to Sandfly Camp

We rose just after dawn. We left the "meeting place" or the Durian Tree Camp today. Before we left, I wrote a note and placed it in a plastic bag next to the big Durian Tree. The note described our situation and our plans in case anyone came across our camp. *Not sure where today went but we zigzagged across the face of the mountain and up and downhill trying to pick up the trail we had come in on. Saw some neat Fungi but didn't stop to take photos.*

Recycling. My thoughts about my place in the forest echoed Hansen's:

> We were frail and insignificant creatures, and at any time we could be swallowed up by the forest. When a plant, animal, or human dies in the rain forest, it soon becomes a part of the forest. Flesh is digested, nutrients recycled, and body moisture reclaimed. (Hansen, 1988, p.124)

One of the ways that systems become resilient is by recycling resources. Mukhtar and I saw examples of this in the jungle by how fungi broke down dead wood and by how termites and millipedes recycled leaf matter. Traveling through Borneo on this trek and trips in the past, I had seen issues posed by the failure of recycling. Biodegradable materials like rattan, bamboo, or leaves that were once used were now being replaced by plastics and metal that could be recycled, however, they could not be recycled in the area. Adizes (1990) and Kimberley and Miles (1980) have explored, through the metaphor of the organizational lifecycle, which leads to growth and what creates or blocks organizational resilience.

» *What are you doing to support the growth and resilience of your organization by reducing or cycling resources?*

» *How can people use their skills in new ways?*

We passed over a collection of fallen timber we recognized but *"... still could not find the original trail we had come into the valley on. It was very confusing and disorienting terrain; very broken with lots of winding creeks and very restricted visibility."* More than once we thought we had found a clearing near the big "Grandfather Tree", a marker we hoped would lead us out, but it turned out to be just us trying to force the ground into a reality we wanted to see. *M really wants to find a red arrow pinned to a tree that he recalls but I think the odds of that are slim. Tried traversing to pick up the trail for the arrow but steep sides of a ravine pushed us upwards to the ridge. Stopped at 1:30 to brew some tea (no breakfast). Walked along the main ridge which is much easier going*

Finally, we *"...sidled across onto a narrow ridge and put a miserable camp on a tiny patch of level ground and got swarmed by sandflies (agas). Lathered on Deet and put on my bug net. Collected wood for a fire but in the end, we didn't try lighting it. Been hearing a number of Hornbill whoop, whoops overhead.* Looking back *I don't think we had any dinner.* Given we did not have any food and the fact that we were having trouble lighting a fire that night, we decided just to minimize energy expenditure. We re-asserted discipline the next night. Mukhtar later told me this was the worst night of the trip for him.

Be lazy. In business, it pays to be efficient, but it often takes effort to get there. In survival situations, you want to conserve energy whenever possible. Being lazy physically does not mean being mentally lazy; or being poorly disciplined. It is about being smart with managing energy. Throughout our trek, I was doing my best to conserve heat and energy by staying dry under the tarp in dry clothes once we were stopped for the night. I tried to keep my feet as dry as I could; I was concerned about getting some version of foot-rot and thus slowing down our travel. In *Back to the Tuichi* Jossi Ghinsberg (1993) describes the debilitating effects of foot-rot resulting from wading many hours along the river during the time he was lost and stranded alone in the Amazonian jungle.

Wet, dirty clothes go on in the morning; dry shorts, t-shirt, and flip-flops go on in the evening. I noticed yesterday that we had been a bit ill-disciplined in our scouting. We had a tendency to take the easy way out and head downhill more than we should have. A tired body wants to take the easy way out, but when we didn't find our back trail, it meant climbing back up again. It was something of a balancing act. We were looking to see if we could find our back trail, but also what we thought might be the head-waters of the river leading to Apauping. Lots of discussions held that day between Mukhtar and I as we fruitlessly searched across the landscape for the best way to go. I kept looking for depressed vegetation, machete marks at eye level, or bent branches. No luck.

DECEMBER 23RD, 2019
Sandfly Camp to Ridgeline Camp

Got away from Sandfly Camp ASAP. More of the same slogging up and down hill and across the hill. One of the markers we were looking for was a red arrow on a tree that we had seen on the way into Durian Camp. No luck. Amazing how everything looks so similar. In the morning we went searching again for the point where we thought we had hit the ridge after coming up from Batu Ning. We were again frustrated in our attempts to find any sign of our old trail.

Towards the end of the day, we had a big decision. We were on the edge of a deep gully. We could drop down into the gully and then re-climb the slope. Our other option was to climb up the ridge to a higher altitude where maybe we could hit a ridge that was also going in what we thought was the correct direction. The day before I had been concerned that we had a tendency to drop down too quickly; that would have us heading towards Long Layu rather than Apauping. I also thought moving back up the ridge, while being harder work, might be safer.

We headed higher up the ridge and found a flattish spot to camp. Secondary forest? Vines with thorns woven like trip wires through the underbrush. A few hundred yards away we found some ponds with water that we carried back to camp and sterilized for drinking and some tea. A tiring day physically and psychologically. No mosquitoes in spite of the standing water. A simple camp. Asleep soon after dark.

DECEMBER 24TH, 2019
'Collapse Camp'

Well today was a little epic. I slept a bit cold last night. We tried to confirm the direction of East from the sunrise this morning but the sun was like weak tea, of limited help. I had seen my shadow once in the last four days for about 15 minutes; even telling basic direction was extremely difficult. I had not brought my compass because no one travels in straight lines in Borneo; we had no useful maps to integrate the compass with. In hindsight a compass or GPS may have at least confirmed the general direction we were heading;

its value for maintaining a bearing would have been limited due to the very broken terrain.

What's Your Compass? Tristan Gooley, in *The Lost Art of Reading Nature' Signs*, wrote that: "Every walk since that one in Borneo I now carry with me an invisible, weightless compass. It has four points on it uphill, downhill, upriver and downriver" (Gooley, 2015, p.324). The rivers have long been the reference points in the jungle. Places were formerly referred to as either upriver or downriver.

It can be very easy to lose confidence when you make a big mistake. Dwelling on the mistake can send you into a negative spiral. Despite the difficulties, Mukhtar and I both expected to succeed in finding a way out of our predicament. I drew on past memories of challenging but successful navigation to bolster my confidence. For example, before GPS systems became available, I had navigated multiple miles in whiteout conditions through cliffs and crevasse-fields in New Zealand's Southern Alps using a compass and a rope to measure bearing and distance. Another time I had navigated 6 miles in a whiteout on the flat featureless ground to hit a 50-foot target, a large boulder.

> Self-esteem acts like an internal compass. …people who expect to fail, do fail, while those that expect to succeed do succeed…. This effect has come to be known as the Wallenda Factor, in memory of Karl Wallenda, who fell from a tightrope after years of success. The story goes that before he fell he was thinking about falling instead of walking. (Mink, Owen & Mink,1993, p. 79)

Some of the ridgelines we followed felt a little like tightropes with steep slopes on either side.

Our plan was still to make our way back to Long Layu, following the markers left by the porters on our way in. *I suggested we drop down to where we had a tea break the day before* back down the ridge, *but we must have missed it. M wanted to drop down into the creek and sidle around to the other side.* It looked like a shortcut. The decision on when and where to take shortcuts would become one of our most common types of decisions as we traded off time, energy, and direction.

> » *How do you decide what shortcuts are appropriate and when to use them?*

I pointed out that we had come from that direction the previous day. So, we headed back up to last night's camp. An hour of energy wasted. After more fruitless searching for our trail back, *we make the decision to abandon trying to find the porters 'trail' from Long Layu and head off on our own. Our biggest discussion yet. We headed up the ridge to avoid dropping into the tempting drainage and found an awesome ridge to follow all the way down to the first creek and nearly to a major river. The ridge was mostly narrow with steep drops on either side but that made it easy to follow. Some places were 4' wide. A few patches needed cutting with the machete but mostly it was quite open with easy travel and not super steep. At the top of the ridge there was actually a path about 4-6' wide but that petered out for some reason.*

High Ground. In the jungle, our view was usually restricted to between 50 to 150 feet. I spent most of the time looking just ahead of my feet to avoid an injury but I also tried to scan the wider landscape. At our high point, sitting on a log, I looked out at the wall of green and pondered our situation. It seemed like we were in a massive 'escape room' exercise. Walls of mountains and walls of vegetation locked us in. It was a fractured landscape. Still, there were some promising exits; there were ridges and spurs running down to apparent river valleys that we hoped would eventually lead to a settled area. I just hoped the exits would not slam shut on us along the way. In military tactics, high ground is highly valued since in looking down you can see and control the whole 'battlefield'. Or at least you can plan with more confidence.

» *What 'high ground' can you find that will offer a more complete perspective on a challenging situation?*

Mukhtar and I could discern two major drainages. One drainage we knew from our general knowledge of the area would eventually lead us to Apauping; this would take us through terrain new to us but past the sites of the abandoned villages of Mangau and Long Tua. The other drainage should lead us back to Long Layu along roughly the route we had come in on. After the villages of Mangau and Long Tua were abandoned in the 1960's Apauping became the furthest village up-river on the Bahau. The people in this area are Leppo Ke Dyak. Between December 2006 when the Apauping's visitor's book was started, (and Dec 14, 2011), only 57 people had come through. Only a handful of these has been foreigners (World Wildlife Fund, 2011). The numbers have increased since then but are still very limited.

Fracture Lines. The ridge acted as a 'fracture line' for us, a critical decision point. Morgan (1988) encourages executives to identify "fracture lines" or breaks in continuity in industry and society. These breaks can arise from events or shifts in such areas as technology, legislation, or economic 'bubbles'. Such shifts have the ability to re-shape societies or industries. From our vantage on the high ground in Borneo, the ridges, spurs, cliffs, and stream junctions formed fracture lines for Mukhtar and me forcing changes in direction or approach. As much as we could, given the limited visibility, we tried to anticipate these fracture lines by reading the general lay of the land and avoiding the fracture lines. We tried to work around geological fracture lines by moving up and around ridges or spurs. Business examples of fracture lines have included the Great Recession, major drops in oil prices, and COVID-19.

On our way to the Durian Tree campsite, the porters had to go searching for the trail a number of times. I later learned that we were not the first to get lost in that area. Gooley (2015) describes getting lost on the way from Long Layu to Apauping and having to retrace their steps to the point at the top of two valleys where they had gone wrong. Reading his tale after my Borneo trek, I couldn't help wondering if I had read his story before the trek, whether I would have done anything differently.

Earlier, Mukhtar and I had decided to try retracing our steps to Long Layu. We had struggled to find any sign of the trail we had come in on; the terrain where we were now was confusing. There was a very diffuse sunrise that morning, the weather remained gloomy and unsettled which limited us in clarifying direction. Mukhtar believed he could identify East from the direction of the sunrise and thus the direction of Apauping. Because the sun was so diffuse, I was not sure whether we were heading for Long Layu or Apauping. I was ok with either direction, as I knew we would eventually reach a village heading downstream. An ancient inscription at the Oracle of Delphi cautions: "Offer a guarantee and disaster threatens." In survival situations as in life hold your assumptions loosely and be willing to adjust or respond differently as the situation changes. It would be a number of days before we could confirm our location. In life and business, you may know you are heading in the right direction before you are able to accurately assess your progress and where you are.

Guessing well and the experience trap. Gonzales (2004) points out the importance of 'guessing well'. Past experiences that ended well, biases in our information processing, information available at the time, and prior training all impact how we perceive situations and make predictions about outcomes. However, our training in making predictions might get us into trouble if that training and our past experiences are not relevant to a new situation. In shifting environments "…what you need is versatility, the ability to perceive what's really happening, and adapt to it" (Gonzales, 2004, p.279).

> » *Where might you be experiencing an 'Experience Trap'?*

> » *What might you need to update in order to make good decisions in an unfamiliar or ambiguous environment?*

I remember heading down a broad spur that narrowed quickly with steep drop-offs on either side. The ridge broadened again, and we came upon some wide trail for a while. We were not off-trail the whole time in our journey. Some paths were surprisingly broad and made for easy travel. Our route at that point reminded me of notes from Hanbury-Tennison's travels in Borneo: "We continued along an easy ridge, following at times a broad trail like a highway, at others cutting across steep hillsides on almost invisible tracks" (2014, p.139). The trails taunted us though; they were just as likely to suddenly stop as to continue. Some of the random trails were likely made by people searching for Gaharu wood. The path would lead a short way and then disappear. The focus of those Gaharu wood gatherers would have been on searching for wood and not on traveling between villages. Mukhtar and I thought initially that the broad trail was a good sign, but when it petered out, we assessed that it had been made by Gaharu wood seekers.

Later that day Mukhtar and I got pushed away from the river as cliffs closed in. We tried to contour around above the cliffs, but even the faces were very steep, so we took a spur up to a high ridge. We climbed uphill a lot. That ridge initially seemed to be paralleling the river and was relatively open. We even found some more trail sections that we suspected had been used by people searching for Gaharu wood. We followed the ridge quite a distance. Eventually, the ridgeline started turning away from the river. We realized we needed to head back towards the river; we started looking for a spur to follow down. Anything we could find was very steep, however, there was some vegetation to hang on to. We alternated between the spurs and dropping into creeks when the spurs got just too steep for safety. A lot of the spurs were of 'double-black diamond' steepness or worse, the mud and loose vegetation added another layer of difficulty. I was getting very tired, both mentally and physically, but the main river finally came into our hearing, and then into our view.

As we headed *down a creek M found a small flat area close to the river and asked how about this for a campsite? As I am climbing up the bank from the river my body started to collapse on me. I felt dizzy, was stumbling and felt like I was going to throw up. I sat down a few times because I was concerned I would fall down. I tried to avoid M seeing me sitting down. I tried to collect some kindling for a fire, but I didn't get much before I start wobbling again and starting to dry heave. M comes running over and sits me down with his pack behind me. He rubbed come kind of oil (minyak tawon) on my limbs, which helped a bit. I just lay down for a while but started to get cold and shiver so I wrapped the space blanket around me as best I could. I started getting cold again, but I was shivering less. I started cramping up in my legs, arms and side. M is doing his best to help me while also setting up camp before dark. I get into dry clothes which helps a lot and now I am writing from a hummock. M is trying to coax a fire to make some tea. Three hard days in a row.*

Margins. Many people often lament the lack of work-life balance. In *Margin: Restoring Emotional, Physical, Financial, and Time Reserves to Overloaded Lives* Swenson (1992) advocates for not filling up every moment, but to keep some reserves. I had pushed the concept of margins right to the limit that day that I nearly collapsed by the river. "In survival situations, people greatly under-estimate the need for rest.... You should operate at about 60% of your normal level of activity" (Gonzales, 2004, p.179).

> » *Where are you pushing your limits in your life in an unhealthy way?*

> » *What do you do to take time to rest and to renew?*

Sustaining a pace. I have had some experiences in knowing how far I can push myself. In my younger days, I ran cross-country, did trail-running, and ran races up to marathon-length. In the Australian Army, I ran a 3000m steeplechase on a day I was sick, had four vaccinations, and had eaten no food. I collapsed five times in the last 100m before I tumbled across the finish line. The middle of a race is always the psychologically most difficult for me. I always start out fast and with enthusiasm and I finish fast with a competitive spirit; however, the discipline of the middle of the race challenges me. *Vires acquires eundo* (Latin—We gather strength as we go). Holiday (2014) makes some useful distinctions: "Persistence is an action. Perseverance is a matter of will. One is energy, the other is endurance" (p.157). Therefore, "knowing that life is a marathon, not a sprint is important. Conserve your energy. Understand that each battle is only one of many and that you can use it to make the next one easier" (Holiday, 2014, p.173).

I rested and recovered that night in the jungle. That day was the middle of the race for me. In some ways I felt stronger the next morning. Pacing is just as important in survival situations as in long projects, or with life transitions. Gonzales (2004, p.134) notes that there is often a 'mad march' to get out of the situation as quickly as possible. Things were not always comfortable for Mukhtar and me during our trek; there was a temptation to move fast and push on until late every day in order to get out of the jungle. Starting too fast can burn a person out in the middle of the race; I re-learned that.

Sometimes to go faster you have to go slower. Most of the time Mukhtar and I tried to do things slowly and steadily especially on the hills to avoid accidents and to avoid overtaxing our muscles. We would stop for camp each day at around 3.30 to give us time to gather firewood and water, set up camp, and to make sure that we were not tiring ourselves out too much each day.

Why is it that some people seem to drive faster in the rain instead of adjusting their speed to the conditions? On Mount Aigulle Rouge in New Zealand I saw firsthand the impacts of 'destination syndrome'. My climbing partners decided to descend an unstable snow slope, which we had all previously commented on adversely.

They were trying to get down more quickly for an evening plane flight. They triggered a large avalanche right below their feet and were very lucky to escape. In the outdoors there are times when rafting to paddle hard to avoid a rapid; other times when hiking, it is best to walk in a slow and measured way. In business speed is important; so is sustained performance.

» *How do you know when to speed up and when to slow down?*

» *Have panicked actions by others, or yourself been risky or unproductive?*

My near collapse was a potential test of trust between Mukhtar and myself. I had let my wanting to be seen as extremely fit and competent get in the way of being honest about just how tired I was; I almost collapsed just after we reached camp. Mukhtar tactfully drew out of me a commitment that we would both keep each other regularly informed of our energy levels. That open conversation helped me to understand when and how I could physically contribute more fully. As an example, I later swam across the river to check for potential food resources in the Conservation Area cabins, thus giving Mukhtar a chance to rest. Mukhtar's graciousness and willingness to assume positive intent helped preserve an effective working relationship between us.

7

PUSHING FORWARD

"Fall seven times, stand up eight"

JAPANESE PROVERB

DECEMBER 25TH, 2019
River Junction Camp on the Sungai Bahau

*W*oke up feeling better after my near collapse yesterday. Good *sleep in the sleeping bag.* Hansen who traveled in the same area offers an appropriate description of the terrain Mukhtar and I were in:

> The forest felt magical and enchanted as long as I was sitting still, but the moment I began walking it became an obstacle course of steep razorback ridges, muddy ravines, fallen trees, slippery buttressed tree roots, impenetrable thickets of undergrowth, and a confusion of wildly twisting rivers running in every direction. All of this was in the shade of the interlocking branches of giant rain forest trees. (1988, p.64)

I don't remember much about this day except that the river gorged us out today. We tried to sidle around but the sides of the river became very steep. Rapids that were too risky to swim or wade blocked the river. We took a spur up, up, up. The spur led to easier travel and topped out on a ridge. The ridge was going roughly our direction, so we kept going for quite a while. Reading Hansen's (2000) descriptions of his journey, now after reflecting back on this time spent in the deep jungle, is for me like looking into a rear-view mirror:

> The rivers wind back and forth in such a way that I would forget in which direction I was going or which river valley we were following. We might cross the same river five times in a day, and I would assume these were five rivers flowing in different directions. When walking…I would often discover that I was walking in the opposite direction to what I had thought. (p.128)

Distractions. It is often not the most difficult terrain that gets people into trouble. My biggest concern on this trek was a distraction that could lead to an injury, especially given the mud, steep slopes, and slippery rocks we were often traversing.

> In the business world distractions are [also] costly: A temporary shift in attention from one task to another— stopping to answer an e-mail or take a phone call, for instance—increases the amount of time necessary to finish the primary task by as much as 25%, a phenomenon known as switching time…It's far more efficient to fully focus for 90 to 120 minutes, take a true break, and then fully focus on the next activity. (Schwartz & McCarthy, 2007, p.72)

Celebrating too soon and blind corners. Innocent-looking river rocks on the creek bottom were covered with a slick invisible film; other times Mukhtar and I had to scramble over boulders, or 'log-roll' over fallen timber. O'Hanlon's (1987) descriptions of the terrain mirrored the experiences Mukhtar and I had. "The river itself began to turn and twist, too, the banks behind us appearing to merge together into one vast and impenetrable thicket, shutting us in from behind just as the trees ahead stepped aside a meager pace or two to let the river swirl down" (p.31). It is natural to want to recognize and celebrate progress but celebrating too soon can sap one's emotional energy. During some of our toughest days, I re-learned this lesson sometimes several times a day. I remember one day in particular when Mukhtar and I started down a steep ridge but were forced into a narrow gully because the ridge just got too steep. The gully was dank and filled with rotting vegetation, thick clay, and pools of fetid-looking water. We scrambled up, over, and around rotting logs expending lots of energy in this very unpleasant environment. The descent seemed to take forever. As we started leveling out, I thought a dip in the vegetation, and seeing a bit more sky indicated that we had reached a major river. My energy and emotional state were more upbeat. However, it was not to be. The terrain was merely the drainage taking another bend. This happened four or five times on the descent that afternoon. Eventually, I had to remind myself that there was a limit to the local relief (the difference in elevation between two points); each turn proved to be a progress point, bringing us closer to the river, our next milestone. During track training sprinters are taught not to celebrate until they have run through the tape. Here is my diary description from that day.

Mukhtar and I passed some trail sections, but eventually this petered out. Realizing we were getting too far from the river, Mukhtar and I looked for a route to descend again. A very steep spur ran out driving us into a gully. Horrible. It seemed to go forever. A mess of mud and rotting tree trunks forcing us to repeatedly scramble up and over, around or under. Dank and gloomy. Finally, that gully ran into a small creek that we waded down the middle of, sliding over rocks. Adidas kampong shoes are good for jungle and for mud and leaf litter, but painful to walk on over rocks. Mukhtar has tougher feet than me, of course, so I am slower through creeks. That creek ran into another creek that we followed downstream. Each time we spotted a clearing that we thought was the junction with the big river it turned out to be another twist in the creek.

» *Have you had a project that faltered right at the end because you celebrated too early?*

Steve Camkin

At least there is no rain today (or this night). The rain we had previously is surprisingly cold. Finally found a scrappy piece of semi-level ground near the junction of the last creek and the big river. Hard day. Left us vowing to try to stay closer to the river. We passed an old, abandoned camp today with two collapsed hummock poles, one split kettle and a collapsed drying rack and we finally had some rice and tea around 7pm. More Hornbills overhead today and some cool orange fungi. We stopped close to dark today at the junction of a small stream and the main river. I am wrapped in my sheet-liner, space blanket and clothes again. I gave my sleeping bag to M. We had ½ cup of rice today and coffee before crashing for the night. I was in bed by 8pm.

DECEMBER 26TH, 2019
Old Temporary Camp on the Sungai Bahau

"Each morning we are born again. What we do today is what matters most" Buddha.

It is easier to press onwards where there is something heroic to do.

> » *How do you stay focused when you are dealing with the routine when your goals seem out of sight?*

We had a ½ cup of rice soup for breakfast this morning with a spice sachet. Mmmm—but that is the end of the solid food. We started off the day wading in the river—looking for flatter ground after yesterday's horrible descent. We geared up to swim if necessary, but I was wary because of the potential loss of heat and risks of injury. There was a very big boulder in the middle of the river with vegetation growing on top of it.

More scrambling around and over ridges as we cut off the bends on some sections of the river. We hit one small creek just before the junction with the big river.

From there things got tricky. Some nasty sidling around the river, steep and long drop-offs or at least muddy slides. I am being as cautious as I can, testing tree roots, my balance etc., and sitting or deliberately sliding often. I might be burning more energy, but I don't want to be the one to create a full-on incident. I am pleased with my focus and feel like I am keeping my emotions in check really well.

Near a steep gully we found some flat ground where we stopped at 3:35pm. The site had been someone else's old temporary camp at the junction of a small stream and the main river. I wrung my socks out in a futile attempt to dry them a little overnight. I tried to shake some of the abrasive mud out too, wary of blisters that could hobble me and slow us down further.

Scanning. One of the things Mukhtar and I were constantly scanning for were good campsites. Level ground, plenty of firewood, and easy access to water can help conserve a lot of energy. Scanning is a skill I learned in the Australian Army and when mountaineering. Our porters had constantly scanned the terrain for signs of food they could take advantage of as well as to look for indistinct paths and the easiest places to travel. Scanning is a 360-degree practice. One needs to look forward in the far distance to look for the general line of where to go. This needs to be balanced with looking forward in the near distance to make tactical decisions. Scanning helps with important decisions such as where to safely enter or exit a muddy creek-line and in looking sideways to search for hooked vines that might catch you as you move through tangled undergrowth.

If I had paid more attention on the way to our Durian Camp, I might have had a better chance of finding the way back to Long Layu. Paying attention to walking your own trail is good advice also for life. How many of us arrive at a point in life and wonder "How did I get here"? I was not the first Westerner to make the same mistake. "I'd been following him, which is never a good idea. I had not walked my own walk, and as a result I was lost" (Gonzales, 2004, p.189). On the trek, Mukhtar and I were navigating, and in life in general, it is useful to pay attention to what you are seeing, to look back occasionally, and to talk about what you are seeing. In doing so you can retrace your steps, if necessary. Look above for changes in the weather or for any potential falling timber in camp.

> » *What are your strategies for scanning your environment for changes, threats, opportunities, or resources?*
>
> » *Do you have blind-spots in any direction?*

Let us not look back to the past with anger, nor towards the future with fear, but look around with awareness (James Thurber).

I think Mukhtar and I figured out the issue with both of us feeling sick yesterday. Too much coffee on an empty stomach. We thought that would give us an energy boost; it was one of the few 'food' items we had. Mukhtar said he felt really hungry today.

Too many resources—binging. One thing Mukhtar and I had a reasonable amount of was coffee sachets with sugar already mixed in. That actually became a problem for both of us. When we ran out of food, we decided to increase our coffee intake drinking it cold from our water bottles. We both found ourselves feeling sick. It was too much on top of an empty stomach, but we felt better once we started diluting it. *Normally when we tried some packet coffee with the sugar in it that perked us up a bit. I have started balancing the coffee with simultaneous sips of water.*

> » *In what areas of your personal life or work life might be better to reduce the consumption of your resources?*

Coping vs. capability building. Coffee did provide Mukhtar and me with a short-term energy fix; what we were lacking was energy to sustain us—fats and proteins. Coffee allowed short-term coping. We needed ways to build our long-term capacity because we now realized we still had days to go before reaching a village.

In business, strategies for short-term coping might including adding more people, dollars, or time to a project. Long term capability building strategies might include process improvement, developing competencies, or organizational alignment efforts. Coping gets you through a short-term crisis; capability building develops your capacity to handle multiple, ongoing challenges.

» *How much of your time is spent just coping?*

» *How much of your time is spent on building capability?*

Mukhtar seems tired today. He is naturally stronger than me, given his occupation. Still, I am very aware *that he is carrying an extra burden both physically in terms of the gear he is carrying, but also mentally.*

» *When you are in a leadership position, and shouldering much of the burden, are you possibly holding others back from them building up their own strengths?*

We passed a Class V or VI waterfall/slide about 20m high that I am betting no other Western traveler has seen. The water in the falls crashed and sparkled, splattering light across the rocks in a dazzling display of scattered energy. I wished I had that energy at that moment. *I think we passed 5 abandoned camps today.* Like the other camps we had passed, these were obviously deserted; however, signs of temporary habitation were plain to see—flattened vegetation, firewood, occasional pieces of plastic, temporary frameworks for shelters (sulaps), or fireplaces. My 'Western' notion of what constitutes 'wilderness' was once again challenged. *Listened to a red hornbill not one of the endangered ones. In fruit season the hornbills knock their heads against the trees to shake fruit down. Mukhtar tried a forest apple today, but they aren't ripe yet. Lots of sidling around the hills today and potential for "Romancing the Stone" type slides down muddy embankments. I did a short swim with my pack across the river and back today to get around a steep, exposed section close to the bank. Mukhtar chose to scramble around the bluff.*

Before I started this portion of our journey, I concocted romantic images in my head of what jungle travel would look like…slowing walking up a sun-dappled creek, gently pushing vines aside, and so on. Some of those elements played out this day, although with a lot less sun. Brief stretches of sunlight filtered through the canopy onto toppled rotting logs with colorful fungi beginning the forest recycling process. Otherwise, the jungle was a shadowy world where light bent weakly around twisted vines, trunks of trees, and a tangle of vegetation scrambling for dominance. "The interwoven tangle of branches, lianas, ferns and orchids found in the Borneo rainforest sustains one of the world's most complex and least-studied ecosystems" (Hansen, 1988, p. 122). The jungle has an astonishing variety of plants and trees and wildlife of wildly varying sizes from bacteria to 2000-pound wild cattle.

The jungle is dynamic. When a tree falls, the sudden clearing is rapidly overtaken by a succession of plants; the tree trunk is consumed by a colorful variety of fungi. Riverbanks are swiftly eroded by the latest flood that brings huge logs tumbling downstream with it. The rain can be torrential one minute, the sun can be blistering hot on the river the next. I had studied complexity theory in graduate school, but here I was experiencing a superb natural example.

Mukhtar was hoping today to get to the point where we should have been dropped but I don't see that happening. I find myself being in the unusual position of being the "realist" rather than the optimist. I wanted to be pleasantly surprised rather than disappointed. James Stockdale, a Medal of Honor recipient, who endured 7 years of captivity and torture during the Vietnam War said: "You must never confuse faith that you will prevail in the end—which you can never afford to lose—with the discipline to confront the most brutal facts of your current reality, whatever they might be." Being resilient in extended situations requires balancing optimism, pragmatism, and realism.

In a discussion with Jim Collins for his book, *Good to Great*, Stockdale speaks about how the optimists fared in camp. The dialogue goes:

> "Who didn't make it out?" "Oh, that's easy," he said. "The optimists."
>
> "The optimists? I don't understand," I said, "now completely confused, given what he'd said a hundred meters earlier."
>
> "The optimists. Oh, they were the ones who said, 'We're going to be out by Christmas.' And Christmas would come, and Christmas would go. Then they'd say, 'We're going to be out by Easter.' And Easter would come, and Easter would go. And then Thanksgiving, and then it would be Christmas again. And they died of a broken heart". (Collogrossi, 2018)

My reading of Stockdale's comments is that to achieve resilience optimism must be balanced with realism. Stockdale also took whatever action he could to help his men and himself exert some control or influence- including instituting exercise plans and changing the guidelines on what information could be shared with the enemy and when. Hope for the best, plan for the worst.

Mukhtar was also hoping to find a plantation where we could grub up some vegetables for soup. It seemed like the jungle had changed little in the last 20 years since O'Hanlon had traveled through the heart of Borneo.

> The jungle around us was secondary jungle, a regrowth of thick vegetation, of tangled young trees and bushes and creepers on ground that had been felled, burned and cleared

for a season's crop of hill paid perhaps ten or fifteen years ago. (O'Hanlon, 1987, p.23)

We did some classic movie-style walking in the riverbed and wading in waist deep water along the edges of rapids. We criss-crossed the river quite a few times looking for the best trail. The trail soon disappeared, and the river choked up with boulders. Several times, we considered crossing the river but judged it too fast for safety in our condition. We also climbed up and over some big logjams today. The river forced us up to the ridge and then we had to do some nasty sidling around the ridge. At 3 pm we came across an old campsite that looked about four months old. We wanted to get another hour of hiking in though, so we pushed on. Maybe we should have stopped earlier for the night since dark arrives at 5.30 in the jungle. Everything turned out fine though.

Mukhtar and I talked about seafood and about other nights where we had camped rough. One of M's favorite foods is Kampong Ayam—wild chicken or village chicken. Mukhtar talked about all the wildlife being captured and killed across Borneo, like pangolin (trenggiling) and porcupine (landak).

DECEMBER 27TH, 2019
Obscure Camp

Fern leaf and garlic powder soup for breakfast. A packet of coffee with the sugar already in it. Mmm. Two kinds of leeches. Plain black and tiger (striped). The tigers are more common here and the hardest to remove. Lots of solutions—scrape, roll them into a ball and flick them away, tobacco, salt, insect repellent. Locals always chop them with a parang. Started hiking at 7.55 am. Took a break at 2pm to make some fern-tip soup. We added a packet of spice mix. Quite tasty. I was skeptical whether the energy invested gathering the fern tips would be worth it, but Mukhtar was quite keen, and it was a good mid-day morale booster. No problems with diarrhea from it like some survival books warn.

Heard deer barking again. More Hornbills. Still, lots of (the world's slowest) roller-coaster hills. Some dodgy footwork along the edge of creek banks and riverbanks but we also had decent trail part of the way.

What not to trust. Kierkergarde said "to dare is to lose one's footing momentarily. Not to dare is to lose oneself." In the jungle, almost everything is rotting. It pays to rely more on your own sense of balance rather than vegetation, but sometimes it is difficult not to reach out. Testing the strength of the branches and vines is highly recommended. One time I was passing a very narrow section of trail about 6 inches wide above a steep slope that dropped about 15 feet. I grabbed two branches at once and started to swing over a gap thinking if one branch broke, I would at least have another to hold. Both broke. Luckily, I was caught up in a bunch of vines before I took a fast slide down the slope. Overall, however, I had been very careful to stay focused and not let my thoughts wander in a way that compromised safety.

My near slide reminded me of a previous climbing trip in Irian Jaya a few years before. A climbing partner and I had been following a river on the approach to Puncak Jaya (Carstenz Peak) in the jungle of Papua. I didn't know it until later, but he had slipped on the muddy trail and was accelerating towards the river 40 feet below and into Class IV rapids when a bunch of tangled vines caught him. My friend had served in Australia's S.A.S. (an elite Army unit) and is a very fit and able guy. Simple missteps can take down even the best men and women.

Moderate attacks of sand flies in the evening until we got the fire going again and after the fire went out. Gus D'Amato, trainer for Heavyweight Boxing Champion Mike Tyson, said, "Fear is like fire. It can cook for you. It can heat your house. Or it can burn you down" (Gonzales, 2004, p.41). For Mukhtar and me, the fire kept the sandflies away but was a psychological boost as well. *Deer barking across the river again. Woodpecker calls. Loud frog calls at night.*

Music and movie themes in my head today... Romancing the Stone slide scene, "slip sliding away" Paul Simon, five weeks in Canungra then off to Nui Dat Red Gum, about Australian soldiers in Vietnam; raindrops keep falling on my head B.J. Thomas; thunder and lightning, very, very frightening Queen. I kill time in my head thinking of things to do when I get back home: catch up with my dearest friend, with other friends and relatives, get more music, write up a blog or story about my Borneo trips, increase revenue from my business, buy a new car, plan my next trip, get into shape again. Food that comes into my mind today ...beef stroganoff, Hungarian goulash, chicken a la king.

There is a cuckoo calling. Can't decide if I am hot or cold. I don't get many hunger pangs anymore. One benefit of no food is that I don't have to go to the bathroom. I occasionally feel like I want to dry heave, I have nausea, and I find myself burping a lot. The biggest issue is loss of power to my legs in the afternoon. Scratches are building up on my hands but there are no out of control infections.

Stopped to camp at 3:50 pm. Swampy area around us. Find a dry spot and flatten out some vegetation for a place to camp. Nothing remarkable or notable about the location so I will call it Obscure Camp. We are still uncertain of our exact location. I try to air out my feet as much as possible during the evenings and so far, that has worked well. Having flip-flops for camp helps. The next section looks flat with trail for a while. Yeah!

8

STUCK IN THE MIDDLE

"If you're going through hell, keep going"
WINSTON CHURCHILL

Dry Camp

*S*tarted the day by wading the river for about 1.5 km—refreshing! Found a big trail after getting out at a pinch point in the river. The trail came to a dead end. Passed two Peacock display areas. My belly is almost totally flat. Good thing I decided to put on some extra weight before I came.

>» *Is your business leaner than it should be? Do you have some fat in reserve for rough times?*

Good news/bad news. We had originally discussed returning to Long Layu and I had thought the drainage we had originally picked was heading back for Long Layu. Mukhtar, more confident than I of the direction we assessed from our first high ridge camp, believed we were headed for Apauping. Neither of us was completely confident. *I've been suspicious the last three days* that the drainage we were following was not the river heading back to Long Layu. The river here is too big compared to where we left it to go to Hillside Camp and it seems like we have been traveling for quite a while. I hadn't raised it with M because by now I feel we are committed to this route anyway. M asked today if I thought we were still on the way to Long Layu and I said I didn't think we were.

A jungle question for you:

> » *What would you do now?*
>
> » *How do you know when to push forward and when to retreat?*

All the signs we saw yesterday gave me confidence that we are getting closer to settled areas. *We passed some small abandoned camps, coffee trees and hit some heavily cut trail, signs of past human activity.* We decided to press on.

Soon after this we broke into a grassy clearing on a bend in the river. I wondered if this was the planned rendezvous point. Next to the river hanging from a tree was a bamboo water container. On it was an inscription to stop killing the animals in the area and the name Apauping. It looked like it was something connected to a wildlife patrol. There was a small noose on the same branch, probably a bird snare. The bamboo container and note confirmed that we were in the drainage leading to Apauping. It was quite a celebration moment.

Bamboo is an iconic image associated with the jungle. I now also associate it with hope. It was the message on the bamboo marker that solidly confirmed we were getting closer to the village of Apauping. Bamboo reminds me to compartmentalize each hour, each day, and whatever challenges I am presented with. Each new day brings a new compartment of challenges. "The human capacity for burden is like bamboo – far more flexible than you'd ever believe at first glance." Jodi Picoult, *My Sister's Keeper*.

Mukhtar and I took the opportunity to wash again while the sun was out.

I had tried to wash each day, but that was not always possible as sometimes the streams were too small. Sometimes I took on the slimy smell of decaying plant matter, mud, and sweat.

We decided to take a rest in the sun, and I lay down on the grass beside the river. Beetles with bright purple wings, Sulphur-yellow butterflies and large black butterflies like orchard swallowtails. On the edge of the grass area were a lot of purple and yellow flowers.

It was probably the most color, apart from the vibrant greens of the jungle, that we had seen since we started our trek.

Clearings. Clearings became important milestones for Mukhtar and me as they stand out in the jungle. When we came to a clearing of any size, we invariably wondered if it was the originally intended meeting spot. Clearings were an indicator to us that we were getting closer to civilization, even if we did not know exactly where we were. Clearings were also a psychological break from the claustrophobia of the forest. They provided a chance to stop, gather our thoughts and take a quick break.

> » *Where have you let things get overgrown in your life?*

> » *What do you do to create 'clearings'? (reflection time and space) for yourself?*

Pushed on after our break but soon spotted another abandoned camp where people had laid down a bed of leaves. They had left behind a grapefruit the size of a loaf of bread. Sweet-

est grapefruit ever! Pushed on from here but we should have stopped. Sometimes a success, or positive indicators, can encourage over-commitment. *Still on very good trail that heads up a ridge with lots of eucalyptus. Saw a Bambura (a mammal like a pig) rush away from us. Some big hills but comparatively very easy footing. Passed a tin sign "left/right" and someone's name carved in a tree. Soon after we passed a direction arrow made of branches. The vegetation on the ridge was more open with some large trees. Unfortunately, the terrain here was drier, and we did not find any water as we climbed the ridge. I have lost one water bottle and have about 2" left in my remaining bottle. M has a little coffee in his bottle. We share the water. Not sure how long we are traveling the ridge and when it will drop back to the river, so we stopped at 4.40 pm high on a ridge for a dry camp.*

Like Hansen, I looked down, searching for any signs of the settlement. "The Kalimantan rain forest was like an uncharted, fathomless, green ocean…" (Hansen, 1988, p. 122). We took out the radio, turned it on, and tried to connect with anyone, but were met again with silence. With nothing to cook we lit a fire simply for the smoke. The locals often toss green wood onto a fire to create smoke to keep insects away; we had no need to search for green wood. It still being the tail end of the rainy season, the wet wood that we found gave off plenty of smoke.

DECEMBER 29TH, 2019
Smokey Ridge Camp

Up early and out by about 8am.

We traveled quite a bit more along a ridgeline before hitting water at a small old camp complete with cup-holders (a bamboo section split four ways) and hummocks fashioned from rice-bags. We stopped to boil water for coffee and to replenish our water, but the wet wood meant it took two hours to get a boil.

Steve Camkin

More big hills today which are tough without energy. This route seems like the world's slowest roller-coaster.

False Summits. One of the challenges with climbing the big hills was the false summits. Nelson Mandela noted "After climbing a great hill, one only finds that there are many more hills to climb."

Our general strategy was to follow the river system downstream; at times the river forced us back onto the ridges to get past rapids or gorges. Other times we came across sections of trail, probably left by Gaharu wood seekers, that cut off major bends in the rivers. In our weakened state uphill climbs quickly burned up our energy reserves. Mukhtar and I were keen to know when we had reached a high point so that we could start the often tricky but less energy-sapping descent. Unfortunately, we encountered many false summits where the climb would flatten out temporarily before resuming upwards. These were familiar for me from past mountaineering expeditions. My strategy in the past has been to remind myself that "at least the false summit means it is not as steep for a while" and "there's a limit to how high this hill can go so this summit is another progress point." Another advantage of the false summits on our Borneo trek was that they gave Mukhtar and me several views of the ranges around us, even those views were restricted. From the high points, we looked for any helpful signs of villages in the distance, but we were met with an endless wall of green. We tried the radio again several times, but with no luck.

> » *What false summits have you encountered in your life?*

> » *How have you handled them in the past and how might you psychologically prepare for them in the future?*

It seems like the route that we are following has taken multiple shortcuts away from the river. There is an adage in survivor lore that you can follow a river downstream to its source, but the reality

is more complicated. Sometimes rapids blocked the rivers we followed. Other times the river was penned in by cliffs. We worked
around those sections, not wanting to commit to the river without
knowing what was waiting further downstream. Each section of the
trail that departed from the river was another decision point. My
feelings echoed those of other survivors. "After a few hours of walk,
however, I once again felt the dread of uncertainty" (Ghinsberg,
p.143). I was concerned we were getting too far away from the river.
Do we follow the longer but easier trail trusting that it would come
back to the river? Do we try to wade and swim down the center of
the river or do we try to hack our way along the edge of the river?

Another jungle question for you:

> *What would you do?*

Trails in Borneo often take short-cuts across the bends in
rivers to save distance. They often involve steep ascents and
descents in and out of the river valley. The idea of swißtchbacks
on a trail is a Western concept. Getting off the river means risking
getting even more lost unless the trail is very clear. Rescuers will
follow the rivers first; it would be much harder for them to spot
us through the dense jungle canopy. For Mukhtar and I following
the river might increase the risk of a slip or fall or getting caught
in a rapid. We judged some of the rapids to be too dangerous to
wade or swim in our weakened state. Even though Mukhtar's
machete marks should have been a clear indicator of our direction
of travel, I also left occasional signs when we changed direction.
I bent some branches in the direction of travel and broke others
branches as markers.

Sometimes, in true survival situations, you may have no
choice but to commit without knowing exactly what is ahead.
Usually, it is better to be able to maintain flexibility and even
backtrack, if necessary. Things went astray in Ghinsberg's (1993)
ordeal when he and his partner committed to rafting a section

of the river that was too strong. They got caught in a canyon, capsized, and could not backtrack.

> » *How much do you stick with a broad strategy and how much do you deviate from that strategy to take advantage of opportunities?*
>
> » *In what situations in your life does it make sense to completely commit?*
>
> » *When does it make sense to maintain flexibility and have a retreat route?*

We crossed several small rivers today. Saw five hornbills today. Two of these flew 20'overhead while we were walking down a creek-line. The sight of these birds always gave me a lift; I envied their ability to rise above everything and fly in a straight line.

Stopped at 3.30 high on a ridge with enough water carried into camp this time. Last night and tonight we slept on the ground under the small orange plastic sheet. We had left our big blue tarp at the supposed rendezvous point because it was too heavy. The smaller tarp is warmer but channels massive amounts of smoke through when we light a fire at the edge of the tarp. Part of the problem -it is hard to find dry wood. It rained about 70% of today. I had been tear-gassed as part of my Army training, but this smoke seemed much worse.

DECEMBER 30TH, 2019
Long Tua 'Hillside' Conservation Camp

Departed around 8 am. Had an enjoyable downhill hike this morning after a few swallows of water. Dry camp last night with just the water we carried in. Open, not too steep terrain. Then a lot of pretty flat creek-bottom with good trail crisscrossing the creek. Good progress. Gloomy in the creeks but no rain. Passed more abandoned camps but they were quite old. Song lyrics in my head today... "someone told me there's a calm before the storm...have you ever seen rain coming down on a sunny day (Creedance Clearwater Revival) *and break on through to the other side"* (The Doors).

We almost lost the trail at a key river crossing point, but Mukhtar went back and re-located the trail. I scouted ahead. I was singing "break on through to the other side" *again when... I noticed a cleared hillside covered in bracken.* I pushed for about 50 feet through the bracken fern which crested above my head *and climbed up a small hill to get a better view. I saw a very large open area and a structure of some description.*

I realized this is the old site of Long Tua; it is now a Conservation Area. In our depleted energy state, it seemed like a steep hike up the grassy hill, but I gained energy from the knowledge that we now have a definite fix on where we are—about 11 miles from Apauping. *Mukhtar and I checked out each of the three structures spread over the hillside hoping to find some left-behind rice but no luck.*

The water tank is also badly contaminated. After we regained some energy, I set off downhill to fetch water from the river. *I might be developing some skills and my balance improving. Later in the day I manage to carry a pot of water 1/2 a mile across several creeks, swampy sections, muddy, root covered trail and back uphill without spilling a drop.*

The open space is quite a contrast to the claustrophobia of the jungle the last few days. There is a good view back to the hills that we came through.

Long Tua is also known as the Bahau grasslands or Padang Rusa (the deer field); herds of wild cattle (betang), deer, and pigs roam the grasslands. *Supposedly we will see lots of wildlife later* tonight. We didn't, probably because of the bright full moon. *There are wild buffalo chips spread across the ground. The nature conservation area is the last home of wild buffalo in Borneo otherwise there are a few in Java. Mukhtar says they are aggressive.* I fleetingly daydream over the possibility of hunting down a buffalo that evening. If I were caught, it would be very expensive steak since *we are in part of a National Park and there is a 100 Billion IR fine plus 10 years jail if you are caught hunting.* I tried bull-riding in my 30's and have been slashed at, stomped on, and rolled in the mud; I did not relish the idea of another close encounter with 2000 lbs. of charging steak and slashing horns, however good the meat might taste.

There is graffiti on the floorboards of the shelters—apparently people come here for visits. It looks like there is a plantation type clearing across the river although it is high up on a hill. M is hopeful we can find some vegetables for soup. My energy is good today. We weigh the likelihood of finding some vegetables there and what effort it would take to swim across and dig or gather them. In my weakened state, it looks like a major climb to the plantation across the river.

We had a bit of bad luck today, or possibly poor planning. While we were taking a rest in one of the shelters, we thought we heard a boat go past down below us. We shouted of course but no response. Perhaps we should have gone down to the river instead of resting. I thought I heard another boat later but it turned out to be just the buzzing of a very large beetle with iridescent purple wings.

Closer to the river there is another collection of about 7 shelters and a cabin built in 2006 by the WWF (World Wildlife Fund, n.d.); no one is there and there was no food left behind. There was some firewood in one of the cabins that I brought back. Some of the buildings are in good repair; others need some maintenance. *A shame. This could be developed as a good remote camp, but it badly needs maintenance.*

Nausea persistent from my empty stomach. At least I haven't had to go to the bathroom for many days. Trying to stay hydrated but not doing a great job today. Barely need to pee. We wandered down to the river later to see if we could find any fruits or vegetables. Found a bunch of Buabarra fruit so we will boil those later. The Buabarra soup had green coffee leaves in it and a little spice packet. The Buabarra is very sour and I could only eat a very small amount.

It looks like instant coffee will be the culinary highlight of tomorrow as well. Hot today. Sunny. It seems like the rainy season might be tapering off. Typical forecasts would have it last a few more weeks. The warm sun felt good as we lay out on the wooden platforms. *5.30 and the sun is due to set. M suggests we stay here for the night and wait for a boat coming upstream. We are in a shelter about 150 m above the river. No wildlife seen yet but this has to be prime country for Rusa (deer).* It is a pleasant temperature and there are no bugs tonight.

Reaching Out. Our brains prefer to focus on the familiar; that often means those things closest to us. Reaching out beyond ourselves is an often-neglected strategy for expanding our resource base.

Reaching out can mean reaching out to the environment or reaching out to others. Part of our reason for leaving Durian Tree Camp after initially staying there for several days had been that it was in a poor location for us to be seen or to reach out. Our line-of-sight radio did not work because we were enclosed in a valley with layers of hills around us. Tall trees dissipated smoke from the fire I tried to keep going and the towering jungle canopy meant visibility was tightly restricted. While traveling, Mukhtar and I looked for open clearings to signal from, or to try the radio from high points or clearings.

During the days on our own, we reached out into the environment looking for food, fire materials, and shelter. A few times while traveling, Mukhtar was able to locate some small Umbud or Rattan roots. They did not contribute many calories but were a psychological boost. On two other occasions, I recognized and gathered fiddle fern tips, the same species I had eaten raw in Australia. We cooked those up as a thin soup with a spice packet. It tasted surprisingly good.

Steve Camkin

We can also reach out to other people. When we first reached the cabins at the Wild Buffalo Conservation Area (Long Tua), we stopped for a while to rest.

I laid out panels in threes (our tarp and clothes) *as a signal in case anyone was flying overhead.* Three of anything (whistle blasts, fires, panels) is recognized as an international distress signal. We also considered using my signal mirror or the Mylar pages in my survival book, but we were well off any flight paths so that opportunity did not present itself. We had tried reaching out on the radio at various high points along our route and here at Long Tua, but the radio was restricted to line of sight and mountains obstructed our signal.

» *How do other people know when you are in need of help?*

» *When do you seek help and when do you decide to persevere on your own?*

More foods I want to eat when I get back: chorizo and eggs, good sausages and eggs, lamb stew, steak and kidney pie, pot roast, lamb shanks, roast pork, beef ribs, pork ribs, beef shanks, hot custard and tinned chocolate cake, Chinese smorgasbord, Mongolian grill, a thick seafood chowder, roast chicken, pork loin, chicken noodle soup or a thick beef-based soup, Ban Mie Vietnamese sandwich, Thai chicken and eggplant curry, chili con carne with noodles instead of rice, other curries especially lamb and beef. I make a mental note to check out the ethnic butchers near home for other meats. Something to drink apart from water, coffee and tea. There is a theme here...lots of meat and fats.

I dwelt on the sensations of warm foods, inhaled smoky flavors, and savored a smorgasbord of textures. I re-played those experiences in my head over and over again. It might seem strange but listing out all the meals I wanted to enjoy was something that built my emotional energy. Instead of deficit thinking my food fantasies gave me a focus for things to look forward to in the future. According to Gonzales (2004) and Ghinsberg (1993), I am not the first 'survivor' to do this. *I watched a full moon rise over the hills and it kept me awake for a while as I pondered what lay ahead for the next few days. We couldn't let our guard down, but I sensed that we were in a new stage in our journey and about to soon transition back to 'civilization'. Tonight, we have a tin roof over us, and a plank floor for the first time instead of a plastic tarp like we have had for the past 16 days.*

DECEMBER 31, 2019
Long Tua Upper Camp to Riverside Campsite Conservation Area (Night 1)

We decided today to move down to a shelter close to the river where any long-tails would pull in to the shore. We gave up staying at the higher location; if anyone was looking for us, they would first check the river systems. Only later would a search and rescue effort be mounted by air. *After moving down to the river, we explored the area close to the shelter but spent most of the day resting. I drop into energy conservation mode trying to doze, swatting the occasional insect, trying to stay hydrated and ignoring the insistent hunger pangs. Another hot, sunny day.*

We started thinking about next steps. The main choice seems to be between staying in place and wait for a rescue, or now that we were so close and in safer country, pushing on to finish the trip ourselves. Emotionally I am ready to push on and finish the trip. Physically I know that it would still be a challenge but very doable. We decided we should take another rest day while deciding on our next steps and trying to rebuild some energy.

Tomorrow we will release an inflated plastic bag into the river with a message in it inside another small plastic bag. It is Mukhtar's creative idea. The plastic bag could drift downriver while we were working on preparations for the last stages of our journey. We agreed it was a long shot, but it would cost us little time or energy to try.

New Year's Eve celebration tonight consisted again, of imagining *more foods I want to eat when I get back: chorizo and eggs, good sausages and eggs, lamb stew, steak and kidney pie, pot roast, lamb shanks, beef ribs, pork ribs, beef shanks, hot custard and tinned chocolate cake, Chinese smorgasbord, Mongolian grill.*

JANUARY 1, 2020
Riverside Camp, Conservation Area (Night 2)

Sand flies bad today. Huddled under the space blanket. We sent our plastic bag with the note downstream this morning. Watched it drift out of sight.

Not sure what message Mukhtar included but he did include an offer of 1M IR, $70 U.S.D., for a boat-ride back to Apauping. I later found out that Mukhtar had written on the note a description of our location, situation, and condition. We placed the note in a small bag and the small bag then went inside a larger white plastic bag. We inflated the bag and sealed it with duct tape. We hoped that our 'message in a bottle' might get picked up by a passing boat if anyone was out hunting or fishing.

Mukhtar mentioned that he had a Python encounter on the Cross-Borneo trail. He was sitting by a small river when a Python head emerged from the water. He thought it was stalking him. Python is considered a delicacy by the Dyak and fetches high prices. This came up in conversation because Mukhtar saw a small python (ular sanca) swimming across the river this morning.

Part of the railing I was leaning against just gave way. It was rotted hollow on the inside by termites. Everything in the jungle is in a constant state of decay or recycling.

> » *What are your support structures? Are they strong and resilient or weak and hollow?*

Broaden your focus. One factor contributing to deficit thinking is the narrowing of focus that often occurs when one is under stress. It is said that our brains use about 20% of our energy and that we are wired to save energy whenever possible (Swaminathan, 2008). The shut-down of creative thinking is one way the brain tries to conserve energy.

My trekking notes record some of the ways we pushed ourselves to think creatively about and experiment with the resources we had. On my packing list that I developed before the trek I had listed fishing hooks and line, however, in the last-minute scramble to finish work and get packed these items dropped off my list.

Trying to figure out if there is any way I can improvise some fishing hooks and line. I have wire in my emergency first aid notebook and there are two reflective Mylar pages I can cut up. I would use floss for line but I cannot find it at the moment. I have found sewing thread and shoelaces, so I have improvised a line, a wire 'hook' and sinker, and a float out of a small plastic bag. The lure is a small strip of Mylar. I tried using this set-up as a throwing line, but the range is too short. I just have it staked to the bank at the edge of a small pool now, a passive, low energy approach. Also, one with a low likelihood of success but it gives me something to do while resting up and while waiting to see if anyone comes by in a boat. Tried modifying the fishing line to float and fly-cast versions but no luck.

No bites from the fish, just from sandflies. Our efforts did however have the benefit of keeping us mentally occupied while we rested.

Locus of Control. Gonzales (2004) suggests that "the Stoics are our best survival instructors. As Epictetus wrote, 'on the occasion of every accident (event) that befalls you, remember to turn to yourself and inquire what power you have for turning it to use'" (p.225). Epictetus was describing what we now often describe as Locus of Control (Rotter, 1966). Locus of Control refers to what an individual perceives they can and cannot control in their lives. People with an internal locus of control believe they can have control over many events in their life. People with a more external locus of control believe that life is more driven by luck or fate. This concept or Covey's (1989) similar concept of Circles of Influence is useful in both change management and survival situations to guide both focus and energy.

What I tried very hard to do during this trek was put the most energy into controlling those things I could control. Discipline helps. We can exercise discipline over what we think by catching unhelpful thoughts and reframing them before they spiral out of control. Initially while trekking I had daydreams of how Mukhtar

Steve Camkin

and I would live off the land, travel swiftly, and be back in a settled area by Christmas. Reality soon set in.

Locus of Control is not just about positive thinking—although positive thinking does help with keeping an eye open for opportunities and having a reason to keep pushing through fatigue, pain, or despair. One way to increase a sense of control is by making goals manageable. I broke large tasks (like climbing a hill) into small goals to give myself a sense of progress and achievement. You can do the same for others that are struggling by recognizing achievement along the way, and not just at the end of the goal (celebrating the small wins).

Mukhtar and I put energy into things we thought we could influence but could not guarantee. We managed our energy carefully. Fishing was a low energy task that also had some mental benefits, but we could not guarantee a catch. When we had arrived at the Long Tua Conservation Area, I had placed out panels in recognized rescue shapes in case a helicopter flew over. Similarly, sending our note downstream in the plastic bags was a low energy activity but had some potential payoff. Our main commodity was energy. Both actions—fishing and putting a message in a plastic float—were unlikely 'moonshots' but both only took a few minutes while we were resting. Both had the potential of a payoff.

We could not control whether searchers came looking for us by boat, on foot, or in the air. However, we could make our best guesses and take actions to influence whether we would be found. It is important to avoid putting energy into activities that are out of your control. The trick becomes knowing what you can and cannot control. My perspective is that we have less control, but more influence than we think in many areas of our life. Gonzales (2004) says that survivors "...deal with what is within their power from moment to moment, hour to hour, day to day" (p.287).

> » *When was a time that you assessed what was in your control and what was not?*

» *Are you focusing your time and energy on things you can control?*

We switched back from 'hunting' to gathering. *Mukhtar cooked up about ¼ cup of fern tips, some Umbud and some of the Buabarra from last night but cut much smaller this time. The Buabarra was much more palatable this time. That was lunch along with ½ cup of coffee.*

Maximize what you have. A clear lesson to remember don't waste resources. In the Kalimantan villages, everything is eaten except the squeal of the pig. I ate pig's blood porridge, monkey tail, deer eyeballs, brains, and pickled pig fat. One tradition I was later introduced to was the equivalent of a drinking competition in a bar but with "shot-glasses" of warm pig's fat. Before improvements in transport "...the oil [had] a much higher value [for trading] than the flesh because it's easy to preserve and transport and because there is a big demand for it in the villages. Locals rated pigs in terms of how many finger widths of fat they have in cross-sections on their back. One finger-width is not so good; four is excellent" (Hansen, 1988, p.160).

My parents and grandparents tell stories from the Depression of the 1930s of making sandwiches with fat drippings and salt and pepper to make do with what they had. Mukhtar and I had made do and had managed to stretch out some small deer bones with a little attached meat into multiple meals. A spice packet with some fern tips and thin slices of Umbud made a surprisingly delicious soup.

I made one exception to not wasting resources. It became the "Buabarra story". After our entry into Apauping, one of the most common questions Mukhtar was asked was, "What does the white guy eat"? Mukhtar bragged about me stating that I ate everything except Buabarra. This would inevitably bring lots of laughter as Buabarra is known for its bitterness. At Long Tua, we had found a large quantity of this very bitter fruit while walking along the river. We washed the mud off, cut them in half and Mukhtar proudly presented me later with Buabarra soup. Buabarra is incredibly astringent and puckered my mouth in an instant. I have eaten insects, raw sea-urchins, muskrat, moose-head, and many other things. I pride myself on a cast-iron stomach and see it as honoring the family I am with, or culture I am in to eat anything put before me. Buabarra defeated me though. I could only eat a few spoonfuls. I judged that effort was not worth the three calories I thought I was ingesting.

Although the story stuck, I am pleased to say that the next night I was able to devour a whole bowl full of Buabarra Soup. We had sliced the fruit much thinner, and it was much easier to swallow. Also, we had mixed the Buabarra fruit slices with some other more pleasant fern tips I had found and some Umbud root that Mukhtar had dug up. The small slices became a metaphor for the whole trek for me. We had been successful and stayed free of injury with many small steps, slicing our days up into manageable pieces.

> » *What unpleasant but necessary situation could you tackle more easily by 'slicing it up' in smaller pieces, or by mixing unpleasant tasks with more pleasant ones?*

After lunch I swam 60' across the river, a little current drifted me downstream above some small rapids. I explored three structures on the other side of the river, again mostly looking for any food left behind. One building is obviously the conservation patrol's building. It had linoleum on the floor, lots of pots, no food. Two brush cutters and generator switches for electricity on the walls. Nothing immediately helpful I thought so I swim back, this time using a length of bamboo for flotation. I used sidestroke at first like I was rescuing the bamboo, then breaststroke.

Later that afternoon Mukhtar and I talked more about our next steps. We estimated that we were about 11 miles upstream from the farming village of Apauping. Farmers in the Apauping area practice swidden farming. I had learned about this practice in high school. In swidden farming land is initially cleared from the primary forest but then is allowed, after a year or several years of use, to lay fallow and renew before use 10-15 years later. Then, swidden, or shifting agriculture was viewed as a cause of deforestation. Today, the amount of deforestation due to swidden is negligible compared to commercial logging and palm oil plantations.

Given the terrain and our weakened state, we anticipated we were 1-2 days travel from Apauping if we decided to push forward. We did not know what the terrain downstream was like. We could see some small rapids just downstream; we did not know if there would be more. The rate of flow downriver was unknown, but we guessed it would slow as the river widened and the land got flatter.

Being on the main river we knew that people would be traveling along with it for hunting or fishing, however, we just did not know when. Given that we were in a conservation area, people would be more likely to hunt downstream, stopping short of where we were. We had also seen graffiti on the buildings in the conservation area and other clues that people came upriver for visits. Because of the

Steve Camkin

huts scattered in the grass clearing and a small vegetable garden, we knew that rangers visited the area, but there was no way of knowing when they would be back.

Given how wide the valley had become, Mukhtar and I anticipated that we could either walk or use the river. No trails were heading downstream from where we were, but trails would become more likely as we got closer to the village. The terrain was still hilly and near the streams, the vegetation was often thicker. Another unknown was whether we would encounter stream-side cliffs that would require scrambling or bypassing as we had previously encountered. We were very hungry, but otherwise in good shape and still mentally focused and alert.

A jungle question for you:

> » *Would you build a raft and float downstream? Follow the river but stay on land? Sit tight and wait for a boat coming upstream?*

And a question for your life:

» *When do you construct and implement plans and when do you wait for others or situations to change?*

We had seen a bamboo grove from the other side of the river; I checked it out on my foray looking for food. I found many usable sections we could use for flotation. *M suggested we make small bamboos rafts and float down to Apauping tomorrow. The packs would go on the rafts and we would swim.* Small rafts would take less effort to build and be more easily maneuvered than larger ones. We could cling onto the rafts while drifting downstream and, if necessary, swim them to the bank to bypass any serious rapids. It would mean losing some heat and energy from being in the water, but the weather was warmer now and we could always move to land and warm up. Forcing a way through the jungle along the banks might use even more energy. Being in the water would be cooler than in the jungle, but we would also need to manage exposure to the sun.

Mukhtar had built bamboo rafts and guided tourists down the Loksado River, a still pristine, mountain area in southeast Kalimantan. I knew basic lashings and had improvised rafts before. We could see at least some small rapids just downstream. There might be more, but I was confident that we could find a way to manage them. I had limited experience on a bamboo raft, however, I have previously taken Swift Water Rescue Courses several times, I am a whitewater kayaker, and I had led raft trips on Class IV water.

Changed batteries in my headlamp as we might try to gig some frogs tonight. Night hunting. Followed a shallow creek line down to the river and back. Saw a tiny frog, which I missed because I threw my bug net over it instead of using my hand to catch it. Otherwise, we mostly saw toads. Lesson learned K.I.S.S. *Heard a civet close to camp tonight. No rain overnight.*

Steve Camkin

9

RE-ENTRY

*"When you're safe at home you wish
you were having an adventure; when you're having
an adventure you wish you were safe at home."*

THORTON WILDER

Apauping

*W*e woke early, as usual, to the sounds of insects and the
jungle coming alive. I had a sense of anticipation knowing
that today would probably be either our last, or second-last day,
of our trek. Watched a troop of Gibbons jumping through trees
in the early morning light.

Returning Home. There seems to be no universally accepted
definition of resilience. The Oxford Dictionary (Lost, n.d.) describes
resilience as "…the capacity to recover quickly from difficulties;
toughness" or "the ability of a substance or object to spring back
into shape; elasticity". When applied to human experience, this
definition seems to be narrow in several ways. We humans do not
just return, like an elastic band, to the same place. Our brains are
'wired' adapt to and incorporate new experiences, especially if those
experiences have strong emotional anchors for us.

The idea of merely returning to a "normal state" or home has been explored in many ways over the centuries by philosophers, actors, and musicians. Heraclitus wrote, around the 5th Century B.C., "You cannot step in the same river twice, for other waters are continually flowing on." In 1940 the book, *You Can't Go Home Again,* by Thomas Wolfe was published. Wolfe's novel explored the theme of the unfair passage of time that prevents the main character from being able to return 'home' or to normalcy. In 2006 Bon Jovi, a singer/song-writer asked "Who says you can't go home?"

Jonathon Look (2017), in a *Forbes* article lamented his inability to return home:

> The forest in East Texas where my childhood friends and I used to hike, play, and build forts is now a strip shopping center. The meadow where we fished in Mr. Parsley's pond is now a drive-through bank. The one-lane road into the woods where my girlfriend and I would sneak away to "go parking" has been leveled and paved to make way for 12 lanes of freeway…[now] the place I once grew up in exists only on maps and in my memories. (https://www.forbes.com/sites/nextavenue/2017/09/24/thomas-wolfe-was-right-you-cant-go-home-again/?sh=70a9db9dee84)

Maybe the better question to ask is: "Do we even want to return to the same place?" The answer may depend on whether we view the new situation as beneficial, or possibly as an interesting challenge for us to think and act differently. It may sound callous, but as the Stanford economist Paul Romer said, "a crisis is a terrible thing to waste". The COVID-19 pandemic, protests, and racial demonstrations in the U.S.A. and around the globe in 2020 have exposed deep rifts in societal views about values, social justice, and equity, about the role of government and about capitalism and whom it serves or does not serve. Do we want to just 'bounce back' to a previous state, as the Oxford Dictionary definition of resilience suggests, or do we want to move to a different place? Leach (2011) suggests that survivors who show resilience in crisis situations go through four key phases—pre-impact, impact, recoil, post-trauma. Do we want to just survive, or do we want to also adapt and thrive? To adapt and thrive, we need to learn from our challenges, individually, organizationally, and as a society.

Mukhtar and I had re-confirmed our decision the night before to float down the river. Mukhtar picked up a length of bamboo for a float and drifted across the river towards the bamboo grove; I swam alongside him. We planned to go back across the river to collect our gear when we had finished building rafts for our packs.

Just after we dragged ourselves out of the water, we heard a long-tail boat heading upriver. *We waved it down and not five minutes later an Indonesian Army patrol boat beached next to us.*

Rescue can sometimes come quickly from unexpected circumstances. When the boat roared into our consciousness and pulled up on the gravel bar, I found myself strangely relieved but also disappointed. *I was a little bit deflated that we would not get to finish in true epic fashion, floating into town on bamboo rafts, but were 'rescued.'* I wished Mukhtar and I could have paddled into the village using our own efforts and, for a brief moment, I even contemplated refusing the offer of help. Selfishly, I saw our story as potentially being a classic heroic story of self-rescue.

There was yet a deeper undercurrent to what I was experiencing. Gonzales (2004, p.63) points out that some survivors label rescue as bad and associate it with loss of pride, shame, and failure. People can undercut their own transition to survival and back to 'normal' if they are unwilling to reach out for help but instead self-isolate. I had experienced this phenomenon in others when I was working in PTSD programs with Vietnam Veterans. Now I was experiencing the temptation not to reach out and accept rescue for myself.

Growing up in Australia, competence, and self-reliance were big values in my family and values which I consciously embraced and cultivated. Self-reliance served me well in the first part of my life. I was seen as very self-confident, responsible; someone who showed a lot of initiative. My self-reliant attitude has served me less well in my personal and professional life as we all become more interconnected and collaborative. Later in my life, this has had the result of sometimes other people in my professional life, and more in my personal life, feeling that either they were not needed, or even wanted. Also, this may have also not allowed me and others to have opportunities to grow and develop personally and professionally.

During the COVID-19 pandemic many people are struggling with whether to remain independent or to accept assistance to get through events that are out of their control. Perhaps we need to do some re-framing on what self-reliance means? Jan Rutherford (2011), the author of *The Littlest Green Beret*, defines self-reliant leadership as "…knowing what questions to ask yourself and then having the courage to answer them and act" (pp.35-36). The actions Rutherford refers to do not preclude asking for appropriate help when necessary. There is value in the fight for 'survival' even if it includes accepting help from others. Furthermore 'failure' can lead to exploration, reflection, and learning. To blot out or discount our 'failures' is to neglect that learning opportunity.

In the end, I knew it would be incredibly ungracious of me not to accept help from the Indonesian Army and the villagers of Apauping. It might have also put in motion a whole series of other unintended consequences. We all exchanged handshakes and there was much smiling and laughter all round.

Mukhtar and I *were soon stuffing ourselves with food the Army Patrol members off-loaded for us -monkey meat that a villager had shot and cooked, an Army MRE* [Meal Ready to Eat] *of curried chicken, rice, deer meat and traditional small, colorful cakes.*

During our lunch-time discussions, we learned that the boat we imagined we had heard while at the upper cabin at Long Tua was indeed carrying villagers traveling upstream. That was a narrow miss to an earlier exit from our situation. No matter, we were safe now. *The telling of our story started to unfold as Mukhtar, and I stuffed ourselves even though we previously swore we wouldn't.* We went quickly, maybe too quickly, from famine to feast. *Another Army boat joined the first one and the soldiers took out some cast nets (jala). Within 15-20 minutes they had 6 small fish and one catfish about 8-10 pounds. The fish were apparently quite expensive elsewhere-132,000 IR* (over $9 USD per pound). *These were gutted and soon spit roasting on a fire.*

The fish were soon demolished, our fingers ripping pieces of the hot flesh from the white bones.

Timing and Resources. Sometimes the availability of resources, rescue, or survival comes down to timing. One of the challenges Mukhtar and I had is that our experience occurred outside the fruit season. We had passed a number of Durian trees that a few weeks later would have been full of fruit.

We were also trekking towards the end of the rainy season; rivers were muddy. In the same area in the dry season, fish are much easier to catch as they are concentrated in the pools. The fish can even be caught using a piece of red thread. Just two weeks later

I watched one of our boatmen land a large fish after "fly-casting" with a coffee bean. There are rhythms in life, as well as in business, around when different types of resources are available.

Later, reading Ghinsberg's (1993) story, I was struck by how much food he had found along the way. He found abundant wild fruits that had dropped from the trees; he managed to kill and eat a snake, ate palm hearts, and came across nests full of bird's eggs. While Mukhtar and I did not find this abundance, my own daydreaming experiences paralleled Ghinsberg's daydreams of food. Like Ghinsberg, I dreamt about gorging myself when food later became available. Still, it was amazing how quickly the detailed drooling I had done over food passed once that immediate need was satiated.

> » *What are the rhythms or seasons in your life?*

> » *In your organization?*

> » *How do you recognize these seasons and adjust to them?*

Cast a wide net or have the right equipment. One of the reasons that the Army Patrol members and local villagers were more successful fishing than us is that they cast a wide net. We were fishing with a single line. Nets were effective in the wet season; our improvised lines were not.

Dick Powell (2015) has a clever book titled *How Not To Lose Your Bass in Business: Business is like fishing*. He presents a parable exploring questions like: Do you have the right equipment? Bait? Place? Time?

Doz and Kosonen describe the core capability of strategic sensitivity as "seeing and framing threats and opportunities in a new way, in time" (Doz & Kosonen, 2006, p.3). One way to do that is to cast a wide net. Organizations that are too internally focused are likely to miss environmental queues or to be too slow to respond to opportunities or threats. Another element of the Doz and Kosonen strategic agility model is resource fluidity—specifically "fast and efficient resource mobilization and redeployment" (Doz & Kosonen, 2006, p.3). Powered boats and casting wide nets provided much faster and more efficient usage of resources than my attempts at fishing using a single line. Powered boats enabled the fishermen to reach parts of the river that we could not and to shift location more easily.

» *What strategies do you or your organization have in place to cast a 'wide net'- to be aware of broader social, political, economic, and environmental queues?*

Check your frames. Another way the brain tries to conserve energy is by creating templates or frames for thinking and action. Past actions, experiences, successes, and failures are incorporated as frames are 'updated'. From my prior experience in Borneo, I knew that locals sometimes stored rice hanging in bags in cabins to keep the food away from rodents. I had swum across the river to the Conservation Area cabins to see if there was any food hanging up in the cabins. That was my frame, or image, of what 'food' would be and what it would look like. Mukhtar had also suggested I keep a lookout for any fruits as these are often planted in small gardens in clearings. I did not see any rice hanging in the cabins, so I went searching for fruit. I reported to Mukhtar that there were small papaya and mango trees, but no fruit.

When Mukhtar later saw this site, he playfully scolded me. I had missed a lot of food sources! Leaves of cassava, lemongrass, sassafras, etc. that we could have used for food. I had told him previously that there were only very small plants. We had missed enjoying a vegetarian meal because my frame of what constituted 'food' was narrow—either rice or fruit. Mukhtar walked me around the garden and showed me the abundance that I had overlooked. Having lived and trekked in the jungle for so many years, he held a different, broader and more useful frame of what constituted food. Later telling stories in Apauping and elsewhere, Mukhtar would gleefully recite how he had missed a great vegetarian meal because I did not recognize all the food around me. An Afghan proverb says, "what you see in yourself is what you see in the world."

Steve Camkin

» *Think about a person you see as a 'hero'- a well-known figure, a parent, a teacher, a friend. What resources does that person draw upon to manage a situation that you are facing now?*

» *What can you do to open up your frame of what constitutes useful and valuable resources?*

» *Are there resources (people, money, assets, strengths) you are not using, and if so, why not?*

A key frame for Mukhtar and I was how we viewed the jungle. We could choose to see the jungle as an adversary, as neutral, or as a place from where we could draw resources.

In his classic book, *The Jungle is Neutral*, Freddy Spencer Chapman relates his experiences of jungle warfare against the Japanese during World War II. He states, 'I met in the jungle six NCOs and men who had been cut off. A month later they were all dead. Yet there was nothing wrong with them' (Spencer Chapman, 2003). The view from Command was that the jungle had killed them. Spencer Chapman disagreed, stating that it was, '…their mental attitude, which was slowly but surely killing them. They were unable to adapt themselves to the new way of life'. Hence his choice of book title: the jungle, Chapman argued, is neither for you nor against you – the jungle is neutral. (Leach, 2011).

» *What frame do you hold about where you work, or about your current situation?*

The others ferried us back across the river and waited while we picked up our packs.

Eventually we loaded into long-tails and headed downstream fast. After days of slow travel, the pace seemed dizzying. *A couple of times we exited the boats and walked around rapids while the soldiers and locals ran the boats through the rapids. Some of the soldiers swam the rapids and raced each other along the river-banks. I felt like my past military experience helped me connect with the soldiers.* The rapids would have been minor, but manageable challenges for us in floating the river. I was envious of the youth and energy of the soldiers. Part of me wanted to get out of the boat and run alongside them. Later I would get compliments for my strength and endurance, especially for my age. However, at the time I felt like an old man. *Long-tails parked along the riverbank, more clearings, and a radio mast were indicators that we were about to land in Apauping.*

» *What might be indicators that you are about to emerge from a challenge?*

Steve Camkin

Concrete stairs reached down to the river from the town. Mukhtar and I disembark and are shepherded through a short section of town to the homestay. Colorful flowers alongside colorful houses. Ubiquitous scrawny chickens scatter as we walk past.

More coffee, and more food as we are invited into a house where we will stay the night. *The army guys say they will be back later.* I went for a short walk up the two streets of town.

Several of the military came back later that evening to the homestay and gave us a friendly 'interrogation'. Mukhtar and I shared documents, passports, and identification, took pictures, they checked the contents of our packs, asked about our past travel and future plans. It was thorough, professional and we all seemed to leave on good terms. Mukhtar is a great storyteller and explains my strange plan to cross Borneo. One police officer, the military commander and three others were there for the second round of conversations. Eventually business wraps up and everyone leaves.

Apauping got motors on boats in the 1960's and phone access in 2016. Apauping was settled over 500 years ago. There is an old abandoned traditional cemetery close by on the banks of the Sungai Bahau.

Found out today that Mangau was the site of the old village where we came across the bamboo water container that confirmed we were on track to Apauping.

The music of the jungle insects, frogs, and birds is replaced by the 'music' of the village. *Next door, the neighbor is playing Indo pop music. In contrast, gongs are clanging, there is traditional music playing at the other end of town. People are in a procession walking through town. It is Tahun Baru, New Year's Eve celebrations, which last five days and five nights. It is bizarre coming out of the relative silence of the jungle to all these sounds. Fireworks and whizz bangs explode later in the evening. Eventually I get to sleep but I wake up several times with painful stomach-aches.*

Re-entry takes time and is a process. We suddenly emerged or were delivered, from our situation. Re-entry is a process, not an event, with multiple stages, learnings, and temporary setbacks. Often, things do not totally improve overnight. Mukhtar and I had been through several rounds of friendly questioning with various military representatives, local police, and local village chiefs. I thought that those meetings were behind us. As our journey continued, we introduced ourselves to the village and traditional Chiefs, and any military or police at each new major village. Our story had spread downstream and across sub-district boundaries.

While I felt some embarrassment at re-living our story, there were moments of humor. I was glad that I had some humorous stories to tell about myself. Humor can be a great way to cut through communication and cultural differences. For Mukhtar and me, humor had also been a great way to maintain and even increase our emotional energy during the trek.

In Panjungan we were again asked about our future plans. The police there had already received a report on our situation. The report, like most stories, had shifted over time in the re-telling. Mukhtar had somehow been 'transformed' into a 20-year-old student that had studied at Monash University in Australia. The attached photo created quite some confusion for a while. In the social media environment of today often 'facts' change; reputations can be made and broken quickly. I happened to check my name on Google shortly after our trek when I got an internet connection. Gone were my previous professional accomplishments; my identity, at least in the social media, was now tightly focused on my getting lost in the jungle.

> *What do you want your reputation or 'brand' to be?*

> *How can you construct or re-construct your brand, if it has been changed or damaged?*

Recovery. For some time, the focus for Mukhtar and me had of necessity been on ourselves and what it would take to successfully emerge from our challenging situation. We did realize, however, that our decisions would have an impact on others. After waiting in Durian Camp, part of our reasoning for attempting to navigate out on our own way had been to reduce the time required for others to find us. This would limit the resources that would need to be invested by rescuers. We were very aware though that if we strayed from the major drainage, that could widen a search area and complicate things even further for those who might be trying to find us.

Crises impact both you and those around you. Change stresses relationships. The immediate concern Mukhtar and I had was for the local people. The Apauping porters in looking for us had clearly invested extra effort to leave very clear signs for us along our likely path.

We had been out of contact with key people personally and professionally for much longer than expected. One of our top priorities, after we got to Apauping, was reconnecting. In one text exchange to my dearest friend on December 16, I had reminded her of my power of attorney information 'just in case'; I shared that she could expect to hear back from me in four or five days. Mukhtar and I emerged from the jungle on January 2nd. She had been texting me all the while wishing me safe travels, a Merry Christmas, and looking forward to us having a Happy New Year; all her texts were met with silence. My first text back to her, on January 2 was "Arrived Apauping. Bit of an epic but everyone ok."

> » *Who do you need to re-connect with?*

> » *What is happening in their lives that you are unaware of?*

> » *Are you aware of what those you care about are experiencing while you are experiencing a personal or professional challenge?*

JANUARY 3, 2020
Apauping

After breakfast I had one more bout of stomach-ache, likely from spicy food after no food for a while.

Steve Camkin

Too many resources—binging again. As Mukhtar and I started to get closer to civilization, we had discussed the risk of binging on too much food too fast. Of course, that resolution lasted about five minutes when the local villagers and military found us. Our food binging on the beach and then in the homestay was just a warm-up of things to come. Apauping was having their week-long New Year's celebration! I was soon dragged into a huge community potluck. Mukhtar declined; he was still feeling quite unwell from breaking our fast. *In the afternoon the owners of the home stay lent me some traditional clothes and I am hustled off to the big celebration at the community hall.*

I am at the head of the procession walking through town and then at the head table. Travelers are treated as honored guests. So many hands to shake and Tahun Baru greetings for the New Year *in both the procession and walking into the community hall. Watch traditional dances and skits. Tons of food of all kinds. Various vegetables, mystery meats and types of cake.* Plates were piled high, pots were simmering, green vegetables shimmered tantalizingly, and a myriad of exotic smells and flavors wafted by.

I had sunk into a sense of luxury and relief—dry shelter, plentiful food, and no-where to struggle to get to—but also reverie. Tonight, any concern was not about physical concerns, but more of a feeling of embarrassment. I leaned into the situation and prepared to make a fool of myself dancing in the streets and doing the Hornbill Dance. *Get dragged up on stage to do the Hornbill dance* in front of about 500 locals. *I do some very bad overacting and get solid applause.* I am later told that making people laugh and feel good is just as appreciated as performing well; another small life lesson for me.

The hornbill dance, the most well-known traditional Dayak dance, is performed in stylized movements of the arms to resemble a flying hornbill. Both men and women wear an adorned headdress, women dancers hold hornbill feathers tied to their hands which will open up when the hands move, while men dancers will hold a shield and a ritual knife. The dance is usually accompanied by sape (traditional Dyak guitar) music. Originally, dances were performed as part of a post-warfare ritual, to greet returning warriors who fought the enemy or came back from successful head-hunting expeditions. Nowadays, dances are commonly featured during the rice harvest season, New Year, and other celebrations, or to greet important visitors to the community. (WWF, n.d.)

Another procession to the end of town and back. More dancing in the streets. Kids climbing trees to watch the procession. Women and kids line the streets popping food morsels into your mouth as you walk by. Often cookies, or 'cake' but it might also be pickled pig's fat. My favorite was Tui, a fermented drink like Arak rice wine. People take turns shepherding me around. Do you mind walking with me? More invites into people's homes and "makan, makan" (eat, eat). Lots of photo requests especially from women, old and young. Amazing inclusion and hospitality. More stories with the Army guys. Popular stories are the hanging bamboo water container and my attempts to eat the Buabarra fruit.

Celebration. Obviously, one of the first things Mukhtar and I did once we were safe was to celebrate. It started at the point we connected on the riverbank with the Apauping villagers and the military and continued through the initial feast on the gravel bar beside the river. Our celebration blended into the afternoon at the homestay and extended into the night when I was invited into the Tahun Baru celebrations. I was struck by the incredibly inclusive way that the whole village had invited a total stranger into their celebrations. Their warmth and inclusiveness were especially noticeable since we had just come in from the jungle, were total newcomers to their village, and had probably caused them some inconvenience.

Part of the celebration for me was the celebration of color. In the jungle, our landscape had been dominated by green vegetation and grey skies until reaching Long Tua, with rare smatterings of color on fungi or insects. In Apauping we saw, in the *traditional art of the Apokayan, fantastic swirls of black, red and white inspired by dragons, and other cultural features, sometimes modified with modern symbols. Houses painted in all colors stood out from the muted tones of the jungle. Plants in vibrant reds, and yellows grew alongside.*

» *How do you celebrate when emerging from a challenge?*

» *How do you encourage others to celebrate when they have come through challenging situations?*

» *How do you involve others in celebrating when people may have had different experiences of a challenge and the different ways they choose to celebrate?*

10

THE NEW NORMAL

"My barn having burned down, I can now see the moon."
MIZUTA MASAHIDE

*W*hat's next? We have survived. We are recovering. What should we do about the longer expedition we started? What is doable now that we are behind our schedule? What do I need to learn from what we have been through?

Purpose. In coming through a challenge, one often asks: what was the purpose of the challenge? Some people pay thousands of dollars to go on quests or undertake programs that include multi-day solo experiences in an attempt to find answers. The Tuareg say: "God has created lands with lakes and rivers for man to live. And the desert so that he can find his soul." Similarly, there are many courses you can take online and thousands of 'life coaches' who will offer to help you find your purpose. I had gotten my experience for free, sort of, with this jungle trek.

Sometimes that purpose only becomes clear as you exit the jungle of your experiences. The Dakota say: "We will be known forever by the tracks we leave." Mukhtar and I encountered clear, broad paths in our journey and some twisting, narrow ones. Some of us are fortunate enough to find a clear purpose through a single

Steve Camkin

event, but for most of us we find our purpose living through the experiences we daily walk through one step at a time. "We often put a lot of energy into doing the big things, but (ideally) we want to feel our purpose all the moments of our life" (Leider, 1977, p.11).

Sometimes the purpose is viewed as a straight and wide path, or as a bright vision. Leider writes:

All life is a spiral of change, a continuous graceful curve towards purpose. There is a definite pattern to it all, and we spend our whole lives seeking that pattern by living with different questions at each age and phase. Searching for the pattern is the heart of our human quest. If we're aware of that pattern, and our place in it, we can identify the best choices to sustain us along the way. (1977, p.25)

I am not sure I agree that the curve is always graceful, but I do agree with Leider's notion that purpose can be evolutionary rather than transformational. A statement by Kristin Zambucka resonated with me in describing the experience I went through in Borneo: "We are all on a spiral path. No growth takes place in a straight line. There will be setbacks along the way. ...There will be shadows, but they will be balanced by patches of light..." (Leider, 1977, p.25).

Why talk about life purpose in a book on resilience? Isn't the point to cultivating resilience survival? Or does resilience have value in itself? Can the process of finding or building resilience help us lead better, more meaningful lives? Potent survival stories are filled with discussions of what purpose people are clinging to, or what people in their lives they are living for. Whether it is the story of Victor Frankl's (2006) search for meaning or any of the adrift, jungle, or mountaineering stories in *Deep Survival* (Gonzales, 2004), having a sense of purpose while going through challenges can help us avoid sliding into a victim mentality. A sense of purpose can help us in weathering adversity. Chief Seattle of the Duwamish tribe said: "When you know who you are; when your mission is clear and you burn with the inner fire of unbreakable will, no cold can touch your heart; no deluge can dampen your purpose. You know that you are alive."

We can also find purpose through re-framing experiences. Much of the trek Mukhtar and I did could be re-framed with 'ifs'. If the trek had gone smoothly—if the porters had met us—if we had sat and passively waited—if one of us had been injured—if I had not met Mukhtar. But here I was doing the Hornbill Dance in front of hundreds of people in the furthest upstream village on the remote Sungai Bahau experiencing one of the most fun-filled nights of my life.

> » *What have been the moments of purpose in your life where you have found or created meaning?*

> » *How do you find meaning and purpose in your day-to-day life rather than just in the mountaintop moments?*

Reestablishing vision. When plans get pushed aside, it is easy in the face of the challenges to question whether those plans are still relevant. Mukhtar and I were recovering, I had lost about 15 to 20 pounds, our schedule had been dramatically impacted, and we would soon find that our story was splashed across international media. Friends and family had been impacted by the loss of contact with us, as well as those who had been out in the jungle searching for us.

> » *A jungle question for you: What would you do now?*

>> a. *Stay a few more days to recover and then head home?*

>> b. *Head out on the next available boat downstream?*

>> c. *Modify the expedition and continue using motorized transport instead of human power?*

>> d. *Continue the expedition under only human power?*

Getting lost did not change the vision Mukhtar and I shared for our longer journey; I saw our setback as a 'side-trip' along the way. After our recovery and celebration in Apauping, we started thinking again about the original vision of the larger journey of traversing Borneo North to South using only human power. We arranged to have some local boatmen take us back up to the gravel beach where we had been found. From there, our plan was to paddle back down to Apauping without motors. It is a strong testament to the grace of the people in Apauping that they did not see our plans as an imposition. I think they saw it as a way to help us achieve our goals while achieving something themselves. They made some money when we hired them, yes, but their pride showing us their skills at 'traditional style' boating without motors shone through as well.

> » *How much grace do you show to people who make mistakes?*
>
> » *Who has shown you grace when you have made mistakes?*

Individual learning. Learning should be in the service of our values, vision, goals, and purpose. Willi Unseold, a member of the first American team to climb Everest, was once asked: "Why don't you stay in the wilderness?" He responded:

Because that isn't where it is at; it's back in the city, back in downtown St. Louis, back in Los Angeles. The final test is whether your experience of the sacred in nature enables you to cope more effectively with the problems of people. …You go to nature for an experience of the sacred…to re-establish your contact with the core of things, where it's really at, in order to enable you to come back to the world of people and operate more effectively. (Phillips, 2013)

Haruki Murakami spoke of the potentially transcendent nature of challenges:

> Once the storm is over, you won't remember how you made it through, how you managed to survive. You won't even be sure, whether the storm is really over. But one thing is certain. When you come out of the storm, you won't be the same person who walked in. That's what this storm's all about. (Goodreads, n.d.)

One of the struggles I am having now in writing this book is how quickly our storm passed, even if it did not seem that way at the time. While Mukhtar and I were in the jungle, our focus was on conserving energy. A lot of what we experienced did not seem at the time worthy of sharing and so my diary notes are scant. Days blended into each other as did the ridges and rivers. Markers to delineate the days were few. Once I had text and phone service again, I was dealing with the details of everyday life—dealing with my phone company and bank, catching up on emails for work, investigating a new car purchase, and catching up with others who were wondering where I had been. After we celebrated in Apauping, we were off again within a couple of days on our longer expedition. When I flew home, I arrived on a Friday and was back at work on the following Monday.

> » *As you are going through the storm, how will you capture the lessons learned before you forget them?*

Learning from success and mistakes. In biological systems organisms that learn from successes in adaptation and resilience go on to reproduce. Darwin is closely associated with the phrase "survival of the fittest". A more complete quote is: "It is not the strongest of the species that survives, nor the most intelligent that survives. It is the one that is most adaptable to change." In our situation, Mukhtar and I tried to identify what was working for us and to find ways to replicate that as we continued. Occasionally switching off the lead, dividing up tasks, and adjusting our route to match our energy levels were some of the small adaptations Mukhtar and I made.

There is much learning to be gained about ourselves from challenges; we can learn how we interact with others from challenges, crises, and adventure. Many have suggested that resilience comes from learning from past challenges. Karen Salmonsohn sums it up as "the most challenging times bring the most empowering lessons." We can learn from the decisions we make. Tim Ferris (2020) points out the importance of making especially good upstream decisions because much extra work and many downstream decisions flow from the initial decisions. Most survival situations require large amounts of energy to successfully navigate the situation. Like the survival stories related by many others, it was the 'upstream' events and decisions that led to much downstream work.

In the safety, survival, and search and rescue literature this phenomenon is often described as a 'chain of events'. The factors creating the chain of events are often some combination of technical, human interaction, and decision-making errors. Sometimes luck (Untung) and timing play a part. Some of the mistakes I made stemmed from early decisions. I made errors both in planning and in execution; there were lessons learned related to these planning and execution mistakes. There were also more general life lessons or refresher courses for me as an individual, but also some different ways of thinking about my work with groups and organizations of different sizes.

"There is a Chinese maxim about a seeker who climbs a very high mountain to ask a sage about the meaning of life. *What is the most important aspect of one's life?* Experience. *How do you get experience?* Good judgment. *How do you get good judgment?* Bad judgment" (Palmer, 1999, p. 50). James Joyce said that "mistakes are the portals of discovery." Some mistakes I made, sometimes more than once were:

Planning and Decision-making

- Overconfidence
- Not asking enough questions
- Not checking if the motivations of all those involved were aligned
- Errors of discipline
- Underutilization of technology
- Personal factors – fear of being embarrassed

Execution

- Navigation
- Resources

Not asking enough questions. I had done a number of prior expeditions in Borneo. Earlier expeditions had all gone well. Perhaps I was over-confident on this trek. I should have asked more 'what-if' questions. What if questions are a great way to proactively break the 'chain of events' that contribute to most survival situations. I should have paid more attention to earlier signals such as the porters from Long Layu taking us by powered boat instead of what I had understood was our agreement to paddle that section of the river. I think I did not question this because I had mentally prepared myself to accept various setbacks along the way given the complexity of the larger expedition I had planned.

I should have asked more questions about the planning around where we would meet up in the middle of the jungle and what were the back-up plans if we did not connect. I should have asked more questions to ensure that both the Apauping and Long Layu porters were operating from the same mental map of the landscape.

There were several factors holding me back from asking more questions. I was not an expert on the terrain, on the language, or on working with the local porters. I have the capacity to ask clarifying questions and should have done so. At the time Mukhtar and I were scrambling to find available porters, I was not as careful as I should have been.

Check that the interests of all those involved are aligned. I made some assumptions about the interests of the porters. I should have asked more questions such as "Why do you want to do this?" and "What concerns do you have about taking on this task?" Previous conversations led me to believe that departing near Christmas would not be an issue. I interpreted those comments broadly; I should have asked more specific questions about impacts on our travel to check that my initial mindset about travel in the region at that time of year was accurate at a local level. Indonesia is mostly Muslim, but the area we were trekking in was a Christian area. It might have been better to slow things down and look for porters after Christmas when people were feeling less rushed.

Under-utilization of technology. I had an emergency beacon I could have brought with me but did not bring. Looking through the rearview mirror, it is possible that a GPS may have helped us in the very late stages of our exit when we finally came into clearings. By then navigation was simple though.

I had justifications for not bringing a GPS:

- The high jungle canopy and steep ravines typically make it very difficult to receive a signal from overhead satellites

- I had tested it out on previous jungle trips and was disappointed with its performance

- I have seen others get into trouble after becoming overly reliant on technology

- It seemed like the far more reliable 'technology' was local knowledge

- The local airline flights imposed extreme weight restrictions; I was trying to just bring items that I would definitely use and which I saw as essential

- I knew we would have a radio with us

- There were no decent maps to pair with the GPS so its value would have been limited.

Lack of attention to detail. I made a few errors when I was especially tired. Luckily, they did not have a big impact. I left my good reading glasses in camp beside my improvised pillow one night and did not remember to pick them up in the morning. Fortunately, I had packed a back-up pair. I also lost a water bottle somewhere along our path. I knew the bottles were not a good fit for the holders on the side of my pack which I had recently purchased in Singapore before the trip. I could have improvised a way to make sure the bottles did not fall off using duct tape, cord, or a vine.

Fortunately, I had another bottle; Mukhtar and I also had other ways of improvising watercarriers. I am generally appropriately patient, but on one occasion I burned one of my liner socks on the fire when I was trying to dry it too quickly. Rookie mistake. I was frustrated with myself for that one. I had extra socks, but my socks were being quickly abraded due to all the mud and water. Having holes in my socks exposed me to an increased risk of blisters, which could have slowed us down. On another occasion when I was feeling very tired, I put my pack down to go off scouting for any trails in the area. It took me a long while to find it again. I was trying to conserve energy, but it probably cost me more energy finding the pack than carrying it while scouting for a trail. Losing the pack would have been a significant issue. The lesson re-learned after taking off my pack and then spending time to find it again was the importance of backup for critical resources.

Navigation. Mukhtar and I had originally planned on returning to Long Layu but instead wound up fortuitously following the drainage into Apauping. When we decided to leave from the high point, we knew there was a risk that we could end up in the wrong drainage. We were willing to accept that risk as either path would eventually get us to safety; we tried lots of navigation techniques before committing. Some of these techniques included scouting, seeking high ground, and trying to use the sun and watches for direction. I do not recall any clear skies and stars we could use to navigate with until we were well into our trek. It is unlikely we would have chosen to travel at night anyway. As I mentioned earlier, there are no usable maps of the area.

Personal factors. Looking back, I think my personality may have impacted my decision to advocate for trying to find our own way out of the situation we were in. We had been faced with a lack of information about our location and whether the Long Layu and Apauping porters would be able to effectively communicate our location. My default had been to advocate for taking action for our own self-rescue.

Being able to avoid repeating mistakes is important not just for survival, but also for learning and personal and professional development. Sometimes we learn at the moment; sometimes we learn by reflecting back on events. Some of the things I learned only became apparent weeks and months later as I tried to unravel the chain of miscommunications, expectations, and decisions that had led to our experience. What had seemed reasonable decisions at the time, based on the information we had, could rightly be judged as errors given hindsight and a wider perspective. Here is some additional perspective, in the form of a timeline, I have patched together after the fact from various pieces of data.

Due to issues of time, translation and physical distance it has taken a while to reconstruct the events that led to our extended time in the jungle. Some aspects are still unclear. For me, the take-away lessons are less about the specifics of who said or did what and more about the general lessons I learned about coordination, expectation setting, and communication clarity and specificity.

When deciding whether to stay at the Durian Tree Camp or to try to navigate our own way out one of our concerns had been that if the porters from Apauping did not realize we were in a different place we might be staying at the Durian Tree Camp, but no one would be looking there. That turned out not to be the case. A number of search groups set out at different times from both Long Layu and Apauping. The fact that none of those search groups came across us earlier, or us across them, can be put down to timing, the difficulty of the terrain, and the dense vegetation. Below is my best attempt at recreating a timeline of events. I apologize if it is not 100% accurate.

16 December 2019

Our contacts at Apauping spoke with the Long Layu porters. The Apauping porters depart to meet us at Pondok Batu.

18 December 2019

Apauping porters arrive at Pondok Batu. Mukhtar and I are not there because we are at Hillside Camp and then Durian Tree Camp.

18-20 December 2019

Apauping Porters waited at Ponduk Batu until 20 December 2019.

19 December 2019

The Long Layu porters leave us at Durian Tree Camp telling us to wait in place until the Apauping porters arrive. In the early afternoon the Long Layu porters return to Long Layu. My recollection is that our planned meeting date with the

Apauping porters was December 19 but since there is a possibility of delays, we know we may have to wait at Ponduk Batu for the porters from Apauping to arrive.

This is where I remain confused, and I have been unable to confirm what happened. Did the Long Layu porters believe they had left us in the correct place and that the Apauping porters would show up later that day or the next morning? It seems possible there was a misinterpretation of which grassy clearing we were all to meet at.

Ponduk Batu has a large grassy clearing and also a rock overhang. I only knew that we were looking for a large grassy clearing so when we later reached Mangau and then Long Tua I thought these may have been the planned meeting point. Ponduk Batu was the correct meeting point. (I remember Mukhtar and me thinking later that the Long Layu porters had thought we were in the right location- but that they may have been mistaken.)

As we started to conclude that we were in the wrong location, Mukhtar and I spent Dec 19-21 trying to find the trail back to Long Layu and waiting to see if the Apauping porters show up at Durian Tree Camp.

20 DECEMBER 2019

Apauping villagers and the Military heard the news that we are missing. I am not sure how this message was passed along. Perhaps one of the Apauping porters returned back to Apauping after they did not locate us at Ponduk Batu.

22 DECEMBER 2019

I left a note on the large Durian Tree saying we are returning to Long Layu Departing at 9 am. I had the date listed incorrectly as Dec 23. We left Durian Tree Camp.

23 December 2019

The Apauping porters run out of food so return back to Apauping. They contacted the Long Layu porters the same day and so both Apauping Porters and Long Layu Porters knew we still are in the jungle.

23 December 2019

We move from Sandfly Camp to 'High Camp'. Mukhtar picks our direction to Apauping based on his reading of the direction of the sun. I was not sure but ok with traveling down either drainage as either direction would take us to a village, either Apauping or Long Layu.

The Long Layu porters got word from people in Apauping that the Apauping porters had not found us.

24 December 2019

Search started. Our Long Layu porters started back to Durian Tree Camp bringing foodstuff/rice. The search party from Long Layu had been unable to find our trail. 6 returned as they were running out of food. 4 continued looking.

25 December 2019

Our Long Layu porters arrive back at Durian Tree Camp. They saw the larger tent was cut and were worried they had been robbed until they found the note that I had left on the large Durian Tree. By the time they had arrived though, we had left. The porters decided to return back to Long Layu but did not find us along the way. They walked in the night to Long Layu.

28 December 2019

Mukhtar asked me if we are still on the correct river, I said I was not sure because of the volume of the river and how long we had been traveling. I was still thinking we were headed for Long Layu. Later that day we found the bamboo sign at Mangau, an old village site. We are now certain we are headed in the direction of Apauping.

29 DECEMBER 2019

A second group from Long Layu with 11 persons joins the search so now the search group is 20 persons.

30 DECEMBER 2019

Traditional Chiefs and Village Chiefs made an official report.

31 DECEMBER 2019

While we are at one of the upper cabins at Long Tua we hear a boat go past but are unable to attract the attention of people in it.

1 JANUARY 2020

The Village Chief of Apauping notifies the Commander of the Apauping post of the local military that we are overdue.

2 JANUARY 2020

The Kepala Desa, Village Head, of Apauping informed the Indonesian Military that we were still missing. The Indonesian Military sent two boats upstream on the Sungai Behau with 8 people and 6 other Apauping residents. Mukhtar and I wave them down at Long Tua.

4 JANUARY 2020

Long Layu receives notification from Apauping that we are in Apauping.

Long Layu searchers return to Long Layu.

The Long Layu search group arrives back at Long Layu.

When deciding whether to stay at the Durian Tree Camp or to try to navigate our own way out, our biggest concern was if the porters from Apauping did not realize we were in a different place; we might be staying at the Durian Tree Camp, but no one would be looking there. That turned out not to be the case. Additionally, if we did walk out on our own, we thought it was likely that we would encounter anyone looking for us as the river valleys would act as a 'funnel'. Part of our motivation had been to get back early before a search party was sent out. Our rate of travel proved slower than expected as we were unable to locate the trail back to Long Layu or Apauping and had to navigate our own way. Surprisingly, we did not encounter any searchers until we were close to the end of our trek. In hindsight, it may have been better to have just stayed where we were at Durian Tree Camp. At least we had implemented a thoughtful and considered plan rather than panicking.

Some life lessons and refresher courses I learned on this trek…

Humility. One of the lessons I re-learned in Indonesia was humility. Humility supports resilience when we are open to learning instead of assuming, we know everything. "When we believe that we have successfully learned a skill…we may see ourselves as stronger or smarter than we are" (DeMoville, 2020, p. 10). In martial arts, this sometimes is called the green belt syndrome. "A Green Belt [is] a rank received that [is] roughly half-way between a beginner's white belt and earning a black belt…The green belt has …an overblown sense of his abilities. Thus, he stepped outside of his center of power" (DeMoville, 2020, pp.11-12). The Tao Te Ching says: "He who is brave in daring will be killed. He who is brave in not daring will survive" (Gonzales, p.198). "Survival instructors refer to that quality of openness as 'humility'" (Gonzales, p.91). I suspect I had grown a little over-confident from prior trips in Indonesia and perhaps failed to show proper respect to the jungle. The wilderness offers us the potential to listen and to learn but only if we are open to it.

I also learned respect through immersion in the Dyak culture and through learning some of the language. In the villages, Mukhtar and I often stayed with either the Traditional or Tribal Chief. When invited into someone's home, shoes are left at the door, you ask 'permission' if crossing through the middle of people, and you make sure feet are not prominent when sitting. You bow over when walking through seated people or stay lower and hold your hand down, to respect someone seated lower or someone older than you. The word maaf (sorry) is used frequently and broadly. Age is a source of respect and wisdom. The head is considered sacred because it is where the spirit resides.

Another way I was humbled was through exposure to the high level of skill of the Dyak people. Their jungle and boating skills are outstanding. Mukhtar and I had encountered both shallow and deep streams in our travels. It reminded me of the concepts of shallow and deep learning outlined by Benet and Benet (2015):

Shallow knowledge is when you have information plus some understanding, meaning and sense-making. To make meaning requires context, thus surface knowledge requires enough context for the knowledge maker to identify cohesion and integration of the information in a manner that makes sense. This meaning can be created via logic, analysis, observation, reflection, and even—to some extent—prediction.

In deep knowledge one has developed and integrated the following seven components: understanding, meaning, insight, creativity, judgment, and the ability to anticipate the outcome of one's actions. Deep knowledge represents the ability to shift your frame of reference as the context and situation shift…Emotions can be a source of deep knowledge (Proceeding) lies in an individual's creativity, intuition, forecasting experience, pattern recognition, and use of stories (also important in shallow situations). This is the realm of the expert. The expert's unconscious has learned to detect patterns and evaluate their importance in anticipating the behavior of situations that are too complex for the conscious mind to understand. (p.3)

The Dyak people that Mukhtar and I encountered had developed deep learning of their environment. Before this trip, I thought I had some jungle knowledge and experience, but in comparison to them, I had merely dipped my toes in the water.

Learning about survival. Gonzales lists 12 things survivors do; my reflections are in brackets or italics:

1. Perceive, believe. "Even in the initial crisis, survivors' perceptions and cognitive functions keep working. They notice the details and may even find something humorous or beautiful…They immediately begin to recognize, acknowledge, and even accept the reality of their situation."

[I remember being struck by the irony of the circumstances when Mukhtar and had first realized we were lost. I teach communication skills for a living and even teach a simple tool, that if I had used it, might have avoided the survival situation. I had a silent chuckle to myself over that failure. The tool is simply using one's fingers as a checklist to ask the questions that a journalist would ask about a story—Who? What? Which? When? Where? Why? How? How Well? And to verify that you have a specific, unambiguous answer for each. Which clearing in the jungle? What time and date will the other porters arrive? How will we all know we are in the agreed location? What is the backup plan if things go awry?]

2. Stay Calm. [One of the initial actions Mukhtar and I had taken had been to calmly assess our situation and then stay in place].

3. Think, analyze, plan. Survivors quickly organize, set up routines, and institute discipline. [Making an inventory of our resources, allocating tasks, keeping a tidy camp, and bathing whenever we had a chance, were examples of actions Mukhtar and I took to establish routines].

4. Take correct, decisive action. (be bold and cautious while carrying out tasks). [I don't think Mukhtar and I did everything correctly, but we made many correct decisions].

5. Celebrate your successes. [This helps to create] "…an ongoing feeling of motivation and preventing the descent into hopelessness". [Mukhtar and I celebrated when we got through the challenging sections, when we found items to eat, and when we reached milestones. And, of course, there was much celebrating in Apauping.

   » *Do you regularly notice when people (including yourself) do things right?*

   » *Do you celebrate small wins as well as significant milestones?*

6. Count your blessings. (Be grateful-you are alive). Find something or someone other than yourself to live for. [Our family and friends were our reasons].

7. Play. "Just as survivors use pattern and rhythm to move forward in the survival voyage, they use the deeper activities of the intellect to stimulate, calm, and entertain the mind."

[I found pleasure in how I moved across the terrain; song lyrics became mantras to stimulate or calm my mind at times. I also envisioned my favorite meals that I would savor when I returned home.

» *What do you use to create a better environment?*

8. See the beauty. (Remember it's a vision quest). "When you see something beautiful, your pupils actually dilate. This appreciation not only relieves stress…it allows you to take in new information more effectively." [On Day 1 of being "lost" I remember being struck by the beauty of some of the tall trees and small ferns along the creek]. Juliane Koepcke fell from the sky over the Peruvian jungle but later said: "I remember thinking that the jungle below looked just like cauliflowers" [Gonzales notes that]. … "She wasn't screaming; she wasn't in a panic. She was in wonder at the world in which she found herself. She was taking it all in, touching her new reality. Checking out her environment while falling. Amazingly cool. (Gonzales, p.172)

» *How could you recognize the beauty and incorporate it in your life and at work?*

Steve Camkin

9. Believe that you will succeed (develop a deep conviction that you'll live). "Survivors admonish themselves to make no more mistakes, to be very careful and to do their very best." [Given our experience base and the fact that both Mukhtar and I knew people would come looking for us at some point, I always thought we would get out alive. It was just a matter of when. My biggest worry was that an injury to one of us that would slow us down].

10. Surrender. Survivors manage pain well. "resignation without giving up." [I accepted that there would be painful and hungry days, but I knew I had past experiences from the military, athletics, and other life experiences that I could draw on].

11. Do whatever is necessary. (be determined, have the will and the skill). [I was confident that Mukhtar and I had both the will and skill]. Survivors "know their abilities and do not over or underestimate them." [Our decision to camp early each day was one way we tried to stay within

our abilities; not swimming down rapids was another. We did underestimate the time it would take to walk out].

12. Never give up. Survivors "accept that the environment (or the business climate or their health) is constantly changing. They pick themselves up and start the whole process over again…" (Gonzales, 2003, p.287). [Mukhtar and I never reached this stage. We had to pick ourselves up multiple times on our journey as we realized our navigation errors and as we encountered obstacles along the way, but we never gave up].

» *Who do you know who might be feeling like they are in a 'survival' situation?*

» *Which of these 12 lessons might be helpful for you to share with them?*

Learning about learning. Without diminishing the pain that comes with crises and challenges, there are also lessons to be learned about how we learn. Matt Walker writes in *Adventure in Everything* about five elements of adventure that can help us in living every day as an adventure, especially in a VUCA environment. Walker argues that "…at the heart of each choice we make is the potential for adventure" (2011, p.7). Mukhtar asked me a number of times while we were trekking whether I was still enjoying the jungle. I can truly say I was in spite of the circumstances. I attribute this in large part to the fact that I was able to view the situation as an adventure.

Walker's five elements of adventure are: high endeavour, uncertain outcome, total commitment, tolerance for adversity, and great companionship. "To aim for a life with high endeavour is to set goals for ourselves that are worthy of our energy, love and passion" (Walker, 2011, p.9). Embracing uncertain outcomes is to recognize that: "…adventure suggests not knowing how something is going to turn out" (Walker, 2011, p.10). When Mukhtar and I headed off from our high point we knew we were headed down one of two major watersheds, but we did not know which one. Initially we did not know the outcome or where would end up. To demonstrate total commitment is to pursue an endeavor "…with flexibility about its outcome, detachment from its results, and complete and total focus on the task at hand" (Walker, 2011, p.11). "Sharing adventures we have the opportunity to give unselfishly, receive sincere feedback, support one another, and work together to reach goals that are unattainable on our own" (Walker, 2011, p.14). It is possible, maybe even probable that I could have eventually found a way out of the jungle on my own. It is much more likely that I would have chosen to stay at Durian Tree Camp and waited for others to find me. Having a great companion in Mukhtar certainly made things a lot easier. Mukhtar was a great and honorable partner in adventure.

11

TAKING IT HOME

"It is not necessary to change. Survival is not mandatory."
W. EDWARDS DEMING

Promoting resilience. Resilience can be looked at from an individual perspective, from a team perspective, or from an organizational/systems perspective. Mukhtar and I had been deeply immersed in a variety of jungle ecological systems; now we were about to re-enter the world of social and cultural systems. Most of us have to demonstrate our resilience in social and cultural settings; we also keep learning (Post COVID-19, Post Great Recession and Post September 11th) that many of our organizations and institutions are more fragile and less resilient than we thought. Based on Mukhtar and my experience, and on research by resilience experts, here are some thoughts on how we can build resilient systems, cultures, and processes in the organizations and institutions in which we operate.

Anticipation, avoidance and control vs. adaptability and resilience. Survival experts and professional guides tend to view survival through two lenses: a preparation and avoidance lens; and a lens focused on harnessing skills and resources if there is a crisis. I have previously mentioned some of the errors I made in antici-

Steve Camkin

pation and avoidance; I have also described some of the thought processes, practices, and tools Mukhtar and I used to maintain our resilience while in the Borneo jungle.

Hilton, Wright and Kiparoglou (2012) in *Building Resilience into Systems* emphasize anticipation, avoidance and control in dealing with crises. They outline a number of considerations to help an organization strengthen its ability to bounce back from challenging circumstances:

- Event anticipation—envisioning what might happen

- Enterprise preparedness—preparing an organization for a range of possible scenarios

- External relationship management—drawing on external resources or advising them of impacts

- Enterprise management—management of people during the crisis.

- Resource management—management of resources (broadly interpreted) during the crisis

- Situational awareness—avoiding tunnel vision; staying attuned to signals in the environment

- Response management—deployment, monitoring, evaluation and adjustment of responses

With regard to all of the above, the enterprise should consider:

- Constraint management—addressing financial, time, regulatory, resource or other constraints

- Strategic management—keeping the strategic picture in mind

- Review, optimization, and improvement—learning for the future

 » *In which of these areas does your organization display strengths and in what areas are there weaknesses?*

One way to avoid some of the stresses of adverse circumstances is by trying to anticipate what could go wrong. This 'pre-mortem' has become increasingly popular in Fortune 500 companies, but as Holiday (2014, p.140) points out, the Stoics developed the technique several thousand years ago. They called it premeditation malorum or premeditation of evils. A similar approach is to use 'black hat thinking' as outlined by Edward De Bono (2016) in *Six Thinking Hats: An essential approach to business management.*

Freeman (2004) offers an alternative viewpoint on building resilience in organizations.

> Systems thought has helped managers anticipate prevent or protect against potential crises, but the modern world also requires resilience, a generalized capacity to cope and act without knowing in advance what one will be called to act upon. Resilience is particularly important strategy for innovative, unique, and transformational organizations that take on inherently unpredictable missions... Of course, it's desirable to anticipate and avert crises whenever possible, but anticipation can be effective only in situations where (1) we know with high probability the worst risks we face and (2) we can apply that knowledge to avoid or mitigate negative outcomes. For most organizations, neither condition applies. (Freeman, 2004, p.1)

Freeman identifies 6 capabilities that support organizations in not only recovering from a crisis but bouncing back even stronger.

- Strong core values and a central purpose that motivate a community to rebuild rapidly

- Psychological containment [management] systems to prevent grief and anxiety from overwhelming rebuilding efforts

- Cognitive capabilities such as an ability to process feedback quickly

- Organic structural characteristics such as replicative abilities, distributed authority, and decentralized structures with redundant nodes

- Attitudes of resilience such as self-responsibility to assume one's own place in the world, rather than to let others dictate it (being proactive allows one to accept the new conditions and move forward effectively)

- Slack resources—money, social capital, and leadership reserves—that can be drawn upon in an emergency. (Freeman, 2004, p.4)

» *Which of these capabilities can your organization draw on in a crisis?*

» *Which might it need to strengthen?*

Resilience is sometimes overlooked as a strategy for securing safety because it strikes managers, administrators, and policymakers as almost irresponsible; they believe they must strive to prevent disasters, not wait to cope with them when they occur. Of course, prevention is preferable to resourceful coping, but that we aim to omniscience (and omnipotence) does not make it so. Many major disasters were never anticipated even as remote possibilities. (Freeman, 2004, p.11)

Some industries and some organizational missions may lend themselves to more stable structures and cultures, however, those are becoming increasingly rare situations in our interconnected world.

> In stable organizations, competitive advantage can be achieved using internally focused strategies. In unpredictable times, organizational survival depends on understanding a broader external ecosystem where purpose and goals are targeted to customer missions, which become a north star to rally leadership and teams around.

> In an Adaptable Organization, understanding the external environment becomes a continuous activity that fuels constant efforts to evolve the business. Adaptable Organizations embed themselves in external networks and position workers to take on the role of "active sensors," always detecting, scanning, and adapting to fluctuating customer needs. Building a culture of constant environmental sensing helps people inside the organization to be open about what they are seeing and how they believe it will impact the organization. It is a stark contrast to the "set it and forget it" strategy and organizational design that traditionally occurred every three to five years. (Rahnema & Murphy, 2020)

> » *What balance of anticipation and prevention vs. adaptability is appropriate for your organization?*

Organizational purpose. Freeman notes that purpose is the 'why' of resilience. Individual survival in crisis situations is more likely when there is a strong reason to live. The 'reason to live' can be seen in organizations as well. As a result of the September 11 attacks, the firm of Sandler- O'Neill lost:

...two thirds of its management committee, 39% of its workforce, and its entire physical plant, [yet] within one year the firm had not only recovered but was doing better than ever. [Freeman and his research colleagues concluded]...the primary source of Sandler O'Neill's remarkable post-attack performance was a compelling invocation of moral purpose. This moral purpose propelled resurgence by directly motivating stakeholders, by enabling outside help, and by unleashing extraordinary physical and psychological resources in concert with 'the pull of opportunity'. (Freeman, 2004, p.4)

Freeman saw the purpose of the firm as not just to make money (Sandler-O'Neill is an investment bank) but a moral purpose: "...to rebuild for their dead colleagues, to protect and provide for their families; and to fight on the front-line in the battle against terrorism ..." (Freeman, 2004, p.4). Even the most purposeful "why" though, needs to be backed up with an effective "how." Sandler-O'Neill used used a number of strategies to manage grief and allow redirection of energy into rebuilding. These included: "...extensive, specialized, on-site counseling services...many opportunities for the expression of grief...leadership actions that demonstrated continuity and engendered identification" (p.6).

> » *Does your organization have a larger purpose over and above making money?*
>
> » *If your organization is emerging from a crisis, are you finding a way to manage grief and a way to connect with a loftier purpose?*

Most efforts to address organizational resilience have emphasized prediction and avoidance of disruptions such as in High-Reliability Organizations [HRO]—nuclear power plants, operating rooms, or air traffic control centers (Weick and Sutcliffe 2001). For some organizations, adaptability and resilience be more important than prediction. For HRO organizations "...the ability to predict what *may* happen is less critical than to detect *actual* small problems and react thoughtfully to prevent them spinning out of control (Freeman, 2004, p.6)." The 'lost in the jungle' situation Mukhtar and I were in could be viewed as possible, but unlikely. Once it happened, our focus was on preventing things from spinning out of control.

Building individual cognitive capabilities. At an individual level, the concept of resilience and the structure of the brain appear to be inter-related with different parts of the brain either aiding or inhibiting resilience. "Brain regions like the pre-frontal cortex and hippocampus and amygdala play roles in emotional regulation and cognitive flexibility, traits that impact resilience" (McEwan & Morrison, 2013). Smaller brain volumes in the pre-frontal cortex and hippocampus are associated with individuals with a history of chronic stress or trauma (Erickson, Leckie, & Weinstein, 2014; Hayes, Hayes, Cadden, & Verfaellie, 2013). In contrast, "...low emotional resilience may correspond with increased or overactive Amydala function" (Leaver et al, 2018). Davidson (2018) found that levels of activation in the pre-frontal cortex of the brain were significantly higher for resilient people. It appears that research from the field of Neuroscience supports ancient wisdom related to the mind-body-spirit connection (Bowirrat et al, 2010) by helping us understand what parts of the brain are involved in generating resilience and how that occurs.

Leadership adaptability. Leadership is central to understanding organizational culture and how an organization responds to transition, change, or crisis. The Center for Creative Leadership identifies three types of leadership adaptability abilities:

1. **Cognitive flexibility**—the ability to use different thinking strategies and mental frameworks.

2. **Emotional flexibility**—the ability to vary one's approach to dealing with emotions and the emotions of others.

3. **Dispositional flexibility**—the ability to remain optimistic and, at the same time, realistic (CCL, n.d.)."

Courage. One starting point in building leadership adaptability for ambiguous situations is having managerial courage. "Rollo May (1975, p.12) says courage is a paradox in that, while we must be fully committed to what we believe in, we must also be aware of the possibility that we may be wrong." (Mink, Owen & Mink, 1993, p.42).

> » *What can you do to promote courage rather than fear?*

> » *How can you balance relating the reality of a situation while still encouraging people?*

Factors and approaches that individuals and organizations can use to promote resilience including:

- Having optimism and a positive outlook (Warner et al., 2012; Southwick & Charney, 2012).

- Having a moral compass (Southwick et al, 2005).

- Utilizing spiritual beliefs and practices (Min et al, 2012).

- Having and utilizing social support (Southwick & Charney, 2012).

- Using humor to help relieve tension and attract social support (Cheung & Yue, 2012).

- Having and maintaining a sense of purpose (Alim et al, 2008).

- Providing social support or seeking social support (Ozbay et al, 2008; Tsai et al, 2012).

- Being altruistic (Southwick et al, 2005).

- Using active coping as opposed to avoidant strategies; psychological and behavioral techniques (Southwick & Charney, 2012; Thabet, 2017; Seligman, 2006).

- Using cognitive reappraisal or reframing (McRae et al., 2012; Frankl, 1946).

- Using constructive sensemaking to examine one's perspective (Weick, 1995).

- Applying mindfulness techniques (Langer, 1989; Thompson, Arnkoff, & Glass, 2011).

- Having an entrepreneurial orientation (Jelinek & Litterer, 1995).

- Examining virtual role systems (Weick 1993).

- Applying adaptive copings strategies (Hobfoll et al., 2007).

- Maintaining an exercise regime. Exercise leads to increased neuroplasticity, reduced inflammation, physical hardiness, and feelings of mastery and self-esteem (Stewart & Yuen, 2011).

- Undergoing hardiness training (Bartone, Eid & Hystad, 2016; Georgoulas-Sherry & Kelly, 2019).

The U.S. Army's Comprehensive Soldier Fitness program attempts to reduce the likelihood of and the impacts of PTSD by "increasing personal strengths, positive emotions, and examining meaning related to a soldier's war-time duties" (Cornum, Matthews, & Seligman, 2011). Research "...examining rates of PTSD in combat-deployed units ...has identified good leadership, unit cohesion, and good morale as potentially protective factors against PTSD, which fits evidence that being able to attach meaning and having a clear adaptive coping strategy promotes resilience" (Hunt, et al, 2014).

» *What capabilities does your organization utilize for building and promoting resilience?*

Individual attitudes. Freeman (2004, p.7) identifies three important individual attitudes that, if embedded in the culture, can promote organizational resilience:

- Self-responsibility. "…Being proactive allows one to accept the new conditions and more forward effectively."

- Attitude of excellence. "Those used to pushing themselves will find it easier to give the push need in a crisis."

- Other orientation. "…provides a purpose, encourages help from others, helps one avoid obsessing about one's own problems, and helps organize response."

» *How are you modeling resilient attitudes and behaviors for those around you?*

Structure. Perrow (2003) suggests that organizations based on organic systems with web-like features rather than mechanical models are more resilient. Organizations can increase their resilience by constructing systems where "…workers [can] perform, when necessary, the tasks of their colleagues (redundancy); an adaptive ability generated from trust, familiar friends and supporters (dormant resources); and a self-regulating work force (decentralized structures with distributed authority)" (Freeman, 2004, p.7).

» *Is your organizational structure designed assuming a stable environment?*

» *Does that structure support stability or resilience?*

» *What is the best future structure for your organization?*

Resources. As illustrated earlier, the Sandler-O'Neill company collectively had a reason to survive, a "why", and a "how" (a plan). They also needed "…resources to withstand the initial blow, and to fuel the early recovery" (Freeman, 2004, p.8). Freeman's research suggests four main types of resources that organizations need in order to recover:

Wealth: Cash, other assets, and the ability to produce wealth

Systems: Internal coordination, processes and procedures, technical expertise

Human Resources: People with requisite skills and extra effort to give (workers who are themselves resilient) …

Network Connections: the quality of relationships with stakeholder…[and] general goodwill towards the [organization] (Freeman, 2004, pp. 8-9).

> » *What resources does your organization have to help it through a major challenge?*
>
> » *What resources do you have to help you personally through a major challenge?*

Organizational Learning. Systems with more diversity of perspectives have more capacity for adaptability and resilience in the face of change. There are big stockpiles of unused, but important and useable knowledge in most families, organizations, and societies.

In my conversations with the Borneo locals and with Mukhtar I had learned how the stories that were passed down by the Leppo Ke Dyak from generation to generation had enabled the following generations to survive and even thrive in their

Steve Camkin

challenging landscape. A 1995 study in Apauping had identified, through interviews with local people and direct observation, that 95 species of plants were being used by the local people for 45 different kinds of diseases such as skin diseases, fever, toothache and stomach-ache (Susiarti, 1995).

The benefit of diverse perspectives in life and business depends though on how well we include and share the rich knowledge brought by that diversity. Another study conducted in Apauping looked at knowledge related to different varieties of rice. Knowledge of the various benefits of different types of rice can help farmers adapt to changes in environmental and climatic conditions.

In 1993 there were 48 households in Apauping. However, when the researcher interviewed 22 farmers, none could identify all the 35 varieties of rice for which that he had collected samples. Even for such a key resource (rice is the dominant source of energy in Dyak culture) knowledge had not been shared across the community. One of the lessons is not being aware that knowledge is available, but learning how that knowledge is generated, shared and maintained. Learning organizations are adaptable and resilient organizations. (Walters, McCay, West & Lee, 2008)

One type of knowledge that apparently had been widely shared was related to soil types. Cairns (2015) notes that:

The Dyak of Apau Ping, in the Upper Bahau River basin, recognize 16 different soil types that offer different properties for certain types of rice" (p.438). In addition to their Swidden practice the Leppo Ke improve food source resilience by spreading supply out across location and time. "… conserv[ing] many plant resources in their fields and home gardens as a strategy to secure their food supplies. Traditional Dyak farming creates a mosaic of different successional stages that not only provide food, but also medicinal plants and those that supply poisons. (Cairns, 2015, p.438)

My experiences also caused me to remember that not all learning is cognitive learning. The Leppo Ke have developed an amazing 'sensory' knowledge base to identify specific plants by properties such as astringency and bitterness (Gollin, 2004). If you have ever tried to climb a slippery notched ironwood ladder or cross a stream on a narrow log bridge, you would appreciate the level of kinesthetic learning that goes into being graceful with those activities.

» *What wisdom is lying unused in your organization?*

» *What processes do you have in place to encourage the generation and sharing of knowledge?*

» *Are there other kinds of learning that your organization should value apart from cognitive learning?*

High ground and swampy lowlands. Learning is key to resilience. Barriers to learning in organizations include gaps between reflection and action, between theory and practice, and between executive and worker level views of the environment. Thompson and Thompson (2015) commenting on Donald Schon's work said that:

Schon drew a distinction between what he called 'high ground' and 'swampy lowlands.' He used the term 'high ground' to refer to the professional knowledge base of theory and research, and he used 'swampy lowlands' to refer to the complex realities of actual practice…High ground implies that the knowledge base of a profession [or industry] gives its practitioners an overview of the terrain in which it operates. The swampy lowlands by contrast, are characterized by uncertainty, 'stickiness' and difficulties in negotiating the complexities of the terrain.

In our trek, Mukhtar and I passed through both high ground and lowland swampy areas. The high ground required effort to get to, but it was often cooler and provided a broader view of the landscape. The swampy lowlands can be hard to move through, are often inhabited by irritating mosquitoes, and are usually places of restricted vision. Even the swamps have their own resource base with different types of vegetation and wildlife. To make your way through the jungle, or any ambiguous situation that requires resilience, you need to connect both the high ground and the swampy lowland.

> » *What are you doing to connect the views and experiences of the high ground and the times slogging through the swamps?*

JANUARY 4, 2019
Apauping

After breakfast we took a Longtail back upriver to Long Tua where we had met the Indonesian Army and the villagers from Apauping. I helped (I think) push and haul the boats up some of the bigger rapids.

We passed the old site of Kabuang which moved to Apauping in 1965 but is still marked on maps. At Long Tua we stopped for a snack and Mukhtar made a point of showing me all the cassava, papaya, lemongrass and pepper leaves that we could have used for food on our last night at Long Tua. I had been looking for fruit, but didn't consider the leaves themselves.

> » *What resources or talents do you overlook because that was not what you were focusing on at the time?*

Long Tua village was abandoned around 1965. The cleared grasslands have now become a refuge for wild buffalo and the area is now a nature conservation area. Long Tua is an impressive lesson in resource management. The locals in Apauping proudly shared their approach to wildlife management. *No hunting is allowed in the traditional reserve. This allows the animal population to grow. Eventually some animals are pushed out of the reserve by overpopulation. These are the animals that are taken by hunters. When fishing, the Apauping residents only take what they can use at the time and no poisons or electric shocks are allowed*. In other parts of Borneo wildlife is being rapidly killed off or losing their habitat. This is accelerating issues around adequate quality food supply for people and contributing to the loss of the traditional way of life. Perhaps one of the saddest things about my journeys through Borneo has been the contrast between the remnants of the once-great old-growth forests and their destruction through logging and replacement with palm oil plantations. To counter this sadness, I took some time while in Borneo to visit places that were emerging success stories for wildlife preservation and conservation.

> » *How might you be squandering resources by not properly managing them?*
>
> » *Does your approach to resources, whether physical, financial or people, show concern for the future?*
>
> » *Is your organization becoming less resilient because of the way it manages its resources?*

While chatting on the riverbank with the locals and the members of the Indonesian army after they had picked us up, I received more lessons in humility. Whatever I thought of my struggles, they pale in contrast to what the Dyak and Penan have long considered part of normal life. *Our boatman mentioned that in his grandfather's day they used to do un-motorized trips from Apauping to Tanjung Selor and back. The trips, to buy Garam (salt) and sell items from Apauping took two months. Occasionally someone would get ill along the way and die. Pushing and pulling the boats up rapids is obviously hard work; it is also potentially dangerous. If you aren't focused and agile there is a risk of getting caught between the boat and a rock or getting a foot entrapped. The locals are wiry and very functionally fit even into their mid to late 60s.*

Mukhtar and I did 'traditional paddling' without motors (dayung) from Long Tua back to Apauping. I was very impressed

with the skills of the boatmen in reading the water and currents.
They make a lot of use of cross-bow draw strokes from the bow
person to nudge the boat into the right section of an eddy or the
stream. When paddling traditional style, the boatmen work with
the hydraulics of the system in which they are operating and not
attempt to power against it.

> » *How can you work with the natural flow of events*
>   *instead of against them to promote positive change?*

It is very difficult paddling from the bottom of the boat, as there
are no seats, so I adopted a Canadian paddling position on my
knees to get a little more height. Needless to say, that is not
comfortable either. We are very spoiled by comfort in the West.

> » *Are you able to be effective even when you are not*
>   *comfortable?*
>
> » *How can you help others be more comfortable when*
>   *they are taking on a new task or skill?*

On the way back to Apauping we passed the Pos (conserva-
tion post) about 1 km downstream from Long Tua. We would
have been quite safe staying in that location as locals come up
that far quite frequently for hunting and fishing. Hunting is not
allowed near the Long Tua Conservation Area and the rapids
create something of a barrier to people going further upstream.
    Our boat had four people, two boatmen, Mukhtar and I. As
we headed downstream we passed a number of other ting-tings.
Lots of people were out hunting and fishing for another big village
party tomorrow night. Ting-ting is another name for a Long-tail
boat-based on the sound their engines make.
    While passing a tributary of the Sungai Bahau *one of our*
boatmen mentioned that two weeks ago they had helped out

a Gaharu wood seeker who had gotten separated from his partner and came down a small river below the Sungai Brau. Again, it seemed we were not the only people to get into difficulties in this area.

It seemed like a quick trip overall for the approximately 18km. We took somewhere between 4 and 4.5 hours including a lunch break.

Back in Apauping Mukhtar and I did a quick trip across the river to visit a 500 year-old family gravesite. I wondered from where the massive stones had been hauled and how. It looked a little like a mini Stonehenge. These stone artifacts were probably carved by the Ngorek people who inhabited the area prior to 1650 and were ancestors to the Kayan people in the region (Puri, 2005, p.45). How had this had been accomplished? Just another example of how much knowledge from the past we have lost.

» *What can you do to ensure that organizational knowledge is not lost, but is transmitted from generation to generation?*

In the afternoon Mukhtar and I went back to the Army outpost to pay our respects, say thank you again, and re-live our story with the Commander and his men. Back at the homestay Indonesian pop music was blaring again in the house next door. It seemed that during Tahun Baru (New Year's festivities) someone was tasked to walk along the "street" to wake people in the morning and also to prevent them from getting to sleep. Some small kids just walked past with a turtle. I wonder if it will become part of the community potluck tomorrow.

I sat up talking with one of the older men in Apauping about old Dyak beliefs, the pre-Dutch and Dutch history of the region, and the WW2 Japanese occupation (the Japanese had a local outpost in the area). The man I was talking with had a clubbed foot and the story was that his mother had violated a local custom by eating wild buffalo meat while pregnant. Deer meat for pregnant women is also apparently a violation of custom, as well as several other foods. Still, in his younger days, this man had made treks of multiple months looking for Gaharu wood and trading in the Apokayan region. The Dyak have traditionally been known throughout Borneo for their Bali akang—their spirit of courage and bravery.

Another Dyak belief… When young men go courting a young woman in another village, if a deer is heard barking, the man must turn back because he will be unsuccessful in his courting of the woman. I also heard a rumor that there was also an increase in deer hunting just before courting season!

Other Dyak beliefs concern when to build a house. Crop planting has traditionally been dictated by the lunar cycle. Planting sticks similar to those used in South America were also used in crop management. When I asked about climate change, a local man said that the seasons (wet/dry cycles) were becoming more variable.

» What are the beliefs in your organization about how things get done?

» Are these beliefs useful or not useful in shaping a resilient culture?

Competency stages. People in crisis situations or professional and personal development often go through four stages of competence, finding ways to move themselves or their teams forward in spite of initial setbacks (Mink, Owen, & Mink, 1993).

Unconscious Incompetence. During the time I was lost in the jungle this stage was represented by when I was unaware I was actually lost. I did not know what I did not know.

Conscious Incompetence. I moved onto this stage when I first realized I was lost. I was aware of my incompetence.

Conscious Competence. Mukhtar and I deliberately made an assessment of our situation, navigated our way out using natural landforms and trails, or used kinds of local woods that are best for a fire.

Unconscious Competence. There were instinctive bush-craft tasks and disciplines that we had both developed through years of expeditions and did without thinking such as purifying water with iodine tablets, rinsing our socks each night, choosing where to set up a fire, or checking for deadfall or other risks before we set up camp.

> » *How can you move from Conscious Incompetence to Conscious Competence?*

> » *What are the best ways to tap into the 'hidden knowledge' of competent others who are no longer aware of why, or how, they do things the way they do?*

January 4 was our last night in Apauping. I was very reluctant to leave. I hope I will return one day. Apauping will always have a very special place in my heart because of the care, generosity, grace, fun, and hospitality of the people. From Apauping Mukhtar and I traveled onward to Long Alango, Punjungan, and Long Jelet, hopefully carrying some of our newly gained skills and knowledge with us. *I watched the ripples from our boat spread out across the river and reach the shore. I hope we have left good ripples.*

I do believe there is opportunity embedded in many adverse situations.

When we tackle obstacles, we find hidden reserves of courage and resilience we did not know we had. And it is only when we are faced with failure do we realize that these resources were always there within us. We only need to find them and move on with our lives. (A.P.J. Abdul Kalam)

Sherwood (2009) conducted research across a wide variety of survival stories looking for common themes. He contends that all of us have some characteristics that we can draw on to improve our potential for survival if indeed a situation is survivable. He identifies five survivors 'types' (Fighter, Believer, Connector, Realist, and Thinker) and 12 characteristics that, if utilized, can improve our chances of survival. Those characteristics are: adaptability, resilience, purpose, tenacity, faith, hope, love, empathy, flow, instinct, intelligence, and ingenuity. He argues that everyone has at least some of these tools for survival even if different individuals have them in different combinations and to differing degrees.

One popular story that deals with finding hidden reserves of courage and resilience is Raiders of The Lost Ark.

"Typically in action films, the hero faces an array of obstacles and setbacks, but largely solves one problem after another, completes one quest after another, defeats one villain after another, and enjoys one victory after another. The structure of Raiders is different. A quick reminder:

- In the opening sequence, Indy (Harrison Ford) obtains the temple idol only to lose it to his rival René Belloq (Paul Freeman).

- In the streets of Cairo, Indy fails to protect his love, Marion Ravenwood (Karen Allen), from being captured (killed, he assumes).

- In the desert, he finds the long-lost Ark of the Covenant, only to have it taken away by Belloq.

- Indy then recovers the Ark only to have it stolen a second time by Belloq, this time at sea.

- On an island, Indy tries to bluff Belloq into thinking he'll blow up the Ark. His bluff fails. Indy is captured.

- The climax of the film literally has its hero tied to a post the entire time. He's completely ineffectual and helpless at a point in the movie where every other action hero is having their greatest moment of struggle and, typically, triumph.

If Indiana Jones had done absolutely nothing, if the famed archeologist had simply stayed home, the Nazis would have met the same fate—losing their lives to ark's wrath. It's pretty rare in action films for the evil arch-villains to have the same outcome as if the hero had done nothing at all.

Indy does succeed in getting the ark back to America, of course, which is crucial. But then Indy loses the ark, once again, when government agents send it to a warehouse and refuse to let him study the object he chased the whole film.

In other words: Indiana Jones spends Raiders failing, getting beat up, and losing every artifact that he risks his life to acquire. And yet, Indiana Jones is considered a great hero. (Hibberd, 2020)

I wish you the best in tapping into your storehouse of inner resilience and finding your heroic self, whatever challenges life throws at you.

Resilience, Persistence and Adaptability

"Don't let the force of an impression when it first hits you knock you off your feet: just say to it: Hold on a moment; let me see who you are and what you represent. Let me put you to the test."

EPICTETUS

"In life our first job is this, to divide and distinguish things into two categories: externals I cannot control, but the choices I make with regard to them I do control. Where will I find good and bad? In me, in my choices."

EPICTETUS

"No matter how much falls on us, we keep plowing ahead. That's the only way to keep the roads clear."

GREG KINCAID

"As with many big changes in life the first step can be the hardest to take"

MORGAN FREEMAN

"Persistence and resilience only come from having been given the chance to work through difficult problems."

GEVER TULLES

"You may have to fight a battle more than once to win it."

MARGARET THATCHER

"It's your reaction to adversity, not adversity itself that determines how your life's story will develop."

DIETER F. UCHTDORF

"Do not judge me by my success, judge me by how many times I fell down and got back up again."

NELSON MANDELA

"Rock bottom became the solid foundation in which I rebuilt my life."

J.K. ROWLING

"On the other side of a storm is the strength that comes from having navigated through it. Raise your sail and begin."

GREGORY S. WILLIAMS

"Our greatest glory is not in never falling, but in rising every time we fall."

CONFUCIUS

"Although the world is full of suffering, it is also full of the overcoming of it."

HELEN KELLER

Steve Camkin

"Resilience is very different than being numb. Resilience means you experience, you feel, you fail, you hurt. You fall. But, you keep going."

YASMIN MOGAHED

"Courage doesn't always roar. Sometimes courage is the quiet voice at the end of the day saying 'I will try again tomorrow.'"

MARY ANNE RADMACHER

"Like tiny seeds with potent power to push through tough ground and become mighty trees, we hold innate reserves of unimaginable strength. We are resilient."

CATHERINE DeVRYE

"No one escapes pain, fear, and suffering. Yet from pain can come wisdom, from fear can come courage, from suffering can come strength—if we have the virtue of resilience."

ERIC GREITENS

"Successful people demonstrate their resilience through their dedication to making progress every day, even if that progress is marginal."

ERIC GREATNESS

"That which does not kill us makes us stronger."

FRIEDRICH NIETZSCHE

"The ultimate value of life depends upon awareness and the power of contemplation rather than upon mere survival."

ARISTOTLE

"Sometimes carrying on, just carrying on, is the superhuman achievement"

ALBERT CAMUS

"Courage doesn't always roar. Sometimes courage is the quiet voice at the end of the day saying, I will try again tomorrow."

MARY ANNE RADMACHER

"To be nobody but yourself in a world that's doing its best to make you somebody else is to fight the hardest battle you are ever going to fight. Never stop fighting."

E. E. CUMMINGS

"Change is inevitable – except from a vending machine."

ROBERT GALLAGHER

"The mind is its own place and can make a heaven of hell and a hell of heaven."

JOHN MILTON

"The person who is not hungry says that the coconut has a hard shell."

AFRICAN TRIBAL SAYING

"There are two ways of exerting one's strength: one is pushing down, the other is pulling up."

BOOKER T. WASHINGTON

"A gem is not polished without friction, nor a person perfected without trials."

CHINESE PROVERB

Steve Camkin

"When you can't change the direction of the wind—adjust your sails."

H. JACKSON BROWN JR.

"You have to look deeper, way below the anger, the hurt, the hate, the jealousy, the self-pity, way down deeper where the dreams lie, on. Find your dream. It's the pursuit of the dream that heals you." Makata Taka Hela At least he wasn't naked, just afraid.

TWEEZERJAM34 TWITTER

Bibliography

Adizes, I. (1990). How companies grow and die and what to do about it. Rutherford, New Jersey: Adizes Institute.

Adventure Alternative. (n.d.). Welcome to Borneo. Retrieved December 31, 2020 from https://www.adventurealternativeborneo.com/

Alim T. N., Feder A., Graves R. E., Wang Y., Weaver J., Westphal M., Alonso, A., Aigbogun, N.U., Smith, B.W., Doublette, J.T., Mellmann, T.A., Lawson, W.B. & Charney, D.S. (2008). Trauma, resilience, and recovery in a high-risk African-American population. Am. J. Psychiatry 165, (12) 1566–1575 10.1176/appi.ajp.2008.07121939 Epub 2008 Nov 17.

ANZAC Portal. (n.d.). The SAS in Borneo. Retrieved 24 May, 2020 from https://anzacportal.dva.gov.au/wars-and-missions/indonesian-confrontation-1963-1966/australian-operations-borneo/sas-borneo

Argyris, C. (1990). 'Overcoming Organizational Defenses: Facilitating Organizational Learning,' 1st Edition, Upper Saddle River, New Jersey: Pearson Education.

Aviation Safety Network. (2006). Flight Safety Database. Retrieved June 3, 2020 from https://www.flightsafety.org

Bartone, P. Eid, J & Hystad, S. (2016). Military Psychology: Concepts, Trends and Interventions, Edition: 1, Chapter: 11, Thousand Oaks: Sage, Editors: N. Maheshwari & V. Kumar, pp.231-248

Benet, A & Benet, D. H. (2009). Managing Self In Troubled Times: Banking on Self-Efficacy. Researchgate Retrieved December 19, 2020 from https://www.researchgate.net/publication/273061340_Managing_self_in_troubled_time_banking_on_self-efficacy

Bennet, G. (1983). Beyond endurance: Facing extreme stress. London: Secker & Warburg

Bennis W. & Thomas R.J., Crucibles of Leadership.HBR Sep 2002 Retrieved from https://hbr.org/2002/09/crucibles-of-leadership

Bhandari, S. (2019). Executive Functioning and Executive Disorder. WebMD Medical Reference. Retrieved December 19, 2020 from https://www.webmd.com/add-adhd/executive-function

Borneo Nature Foundation. (2013). Species Saturday #22: Fire ants. July 26, 2013. Retrieved July 26, 2020 from http://www.borneonature-foundation.org/en/species-saturday/species-saturday-22-fire-ants/

Bowirrat, A., Chen, T.J.H., Blum, K., Madigan, M., Bailey, J.A., Chen, A.L.C., Downs, B.W., Braveman, E.R., Radi, S., Waite, R.L., Kerner, M., Giordano, J., Morse, S., Oscar-Berman, M. & Gold, M. (2010). Neuro-psychopharmacogenetics and Neurological Antecedents of Post-traumatic Stress Disorder: Unlocking the Mysteries of Resilience and Vulnerability. Curr Neuropharmacol. 2010 Dec; 8(4): 335–Retrieved 6 June, 6, 2020 from 358. doi: 10.2174/15701591079335812 3 https://www.ncbi.nlm.nih.gov/pmc/articles/PMC3080591/

Bradberry, T. & Greaves, J. (2009). Emotional Intelligence 2.0. San Diego: Talentsmart.

Cairns, M. (ed.). (2015). Shifting Cultivation and Environmental Change: Indigenous people, agriculture and forest conservation. Abingdon, U.K: Routledge.

Center For Creative Leadership. (n.d.). Adapting to Change Requires Flexibility. Retrieved June 4, 2020 from https://www.ccl.org/articles/leading-effectively-articles/adaptability-1-idea-3-facts-5-tips/

Cheung C. K., Yue X. D. (2012). Sojourn students' humor styles as buffers to achieve resilience. Int. J. Intercult. Relat. 36, 353–364

Collogrossi, M. (2018). Stockdale Paradox: Why confronting reality is vital to success. Big Think. 15 November, 2018 Retrieved July 30, 2020 from https://bigthink.com/personal-growth/stockdale-paradox-confronting-reality-vital-success?rebelltitem=1#rebelltitem1

Cornum, R. Matthews, M.D. & Seligman, M.E.P. (2011). Comprehensive Soldier Fitness: Building Resilience in a challenging institutional context. American Psychologist, 66(1), 4–9. Retrieved June 6, 2020 from https://doi.org/10.1037/a0021420https://psycnet.apa.org/doi-Landing?doi=10.1037%2Fa0021420

Corrigan, P.& Fitzmaurice, L. (2012). Man Lost 20 days in Jungle Escapes. St Louis Dispatch Feb 15,2012 Retrieved June 29, 2020 from https://www.questia.com/newspaper/1P2-32821788/man-lost-

20-days-in-jungle-escapes

Coutu, D. (2010). How Resilience Works in On Managing Yourself. HBR, Boston: HBR Press.

Covey, S.R. (1989). The Seven Habits of Highly Effective People: Powerful lessons in personal change. New York: Simon & Schuster.

Davidson, R. (2018). The Emotional Life in Your Brain. In The Neuroscience of Building a Resilient Brain Retrieved August 5, 2020 from https://thebestbrainpossible.com/neuroscience-resilient-brainstress

Davis, W. (1991). The Penan: Community in the Rainforest. Living Together (IC #29) Summer 1991, p.48. Context Institute. Retrieved June 4, 2020 from https://www.context.org/iclib/ic29/davis/

De Bono, E. (1981). Atlas of Management Thinking. London: Temple Smith.

De Bono, E. (2016). Six Thinking Hats: An essential approach to business management. New York: Penguin.

DeMoville, B. (2020). Nine Principles of The Shadow Warrior: Empower yourself for the fight of your life. Waco, Texas: Honshin Productions.

Doz, Y. & Kosonen, M. (2006). Fostering Strategic Agility: In search for renewed growth. CKIR Workshop Aug 29, 2006 INSEAD Retrieved June 6, 2020 from http://agilityconsulting.com/resources/SAI/INSEADAgility1.pdf

Eede, J. (2013). Celebrating the Indigenous Skills of Tribes. National Geographic Society Newsroom. August 14, 2013. Retrieved July 5, 2020 from https://blog.nationalgeographic.org/2013/08/14/celebrating-the-ingenious-skills-of-tribes/

Erickson, K.I., Leckie, R.L. & Weinstein, A.M. (2014). Physical Activity, fitness and gray matter volume. Neurobiology of Aging. Vol. 35, Supplement 2, Sept 2014. pp.20-28.

Ferris, T. (2020). Finding the One Decision That Removes 100 Decisions (or, Why I'm Reading No New Books in 2020). The Tim Ferris Blog. Jan 20, 2020. Retrieved 4 June 4, 2020 from https://tim.blog/2020/01/20/one-decision-that-removes-100-decisions/

Frankl, V.E. (1946). Man's Search for Meaning. Vienna: Beacon Press.

Freeman, S.F. (2004). Beyond Traditional Systems Thinking: Resilience as a strategy for security and sustainability. 3rd International Conference on Systems Thinking in Management Session on Sustainability Philadelphia, 20 May, 2004

Georgoulas-Sherry, V.& Kelly, D.R. (2019). Resilience, Grit, and Hardiness: Determining the Relationships amongst these Constructs through Structural Equation Modeling Techniques. Journal of Positive Psychology & Wellbeing 2019, Vol. 3, No. 2, 165 –178

Ghinsberg, J. (1993). Back from Tuchi: The harrowing life-and-death story of survival in the Amazon Rainforest. New York: Random House.

Gollin, L. (2004). Subtle and Profound Sensory Attributes of Medicinal Plants Among the Kenyah Leppo Ke People of East Kalimantan, Borneo. Journal of Ethnobiology 24 (2):173-201 Fall/Winter 2004 Retrieved 26 July, 26, 2020 from pdf.semanticscholar.org

Gonzales, L. (2003). Deep Survival: Who lives, who dies and why. New York: Norton.

Goodman, J., Schlossberg, N. K., & Anderson, M. L. (2006). *Counseling adults in transition: Linking practice with theory* (3rd ed.). Springer Publishing Co.

Goodreads. (n.d.). www.goodreads.com Retrieved January 2, 2021 from https://www.goodreads.com/quotes/315361-and-once-the-storm-is-over-you-won-t-remember-how

Gooley, T. (2015). The Lost Art of Reading Nature's Signs: Use outdoor clues to find your way. New York: Experiment.

Gossamergear. (2019). How Search and Rescue Changed My Survival Mindset. Retrieved January 2, 2021 from https://www.gossamergear.com/blogs/our-blog/search-and-rescue

Half, R. (n.d.). allauthor.com Retrieved Dec 31, 2020 from https://allauthor.com/quotes/1936/

Hanbury-Tennison, R. (2017). Finding Eden: A journey into the Heart of Borneo. New York: I.B. Taurus.

Hansen, E. (1988). Stranger in the Forest: On foot across Borneo. Boston: MA: Houghton-Mifflin.

Harrison, T. (1938). 'Remembered Jungle', in Tom Harrison (ed.), Borneo Jungle: An Account of the Oxford University Expedition of 1932 (London: Lindsay Drummond, 1938) in Hanbury-Tennison, R. (2017) p.9 Finding Eden: A Journey into the Heart of Borneo. London: I.B. Taurus.

Hayes, S. M., Hayes, J. P., Cadden, M., & Verfaellie, M. (2013). A review of cardiorespiratory fitness-related neuroplasticity in the aging brain. Frontiers in Aging Neuroscience, 5, Article 31. Retrieved June 6, 2020 from https://doi.org/10.3389/fnagi.2013.00031

Hibberd, J., (2020). What Indiana Jones Can Teach Us During Hard Times: A brief parable inspired by 'Raiders of the Lost Ark'. July 31st, 2020 Retrieved August 17, 2020 from https://ew.com/movies/indiana-jones-raiders-parable/

Hilton, J., Wright., C & Kiparoglou, V. (2012). Building resilience into systems. IEEE International Systems Conference, Proceedings 2012

Hobfoll, S.E., Bell, C.C. Bryant, R. & Watson, P.J. (2007). Five Essential Elements of Immediate and Mid-Term Mass Trauma Intervention: Empirical Evidence. Psychiatry Interpersonal & Biological Processes *70(4):283-315;* discussion 316-69 ·February 2007 Retrieved June 6, 2020 from https://www.researchgate.net/publication/5668133_Five_Essential_Elements_of_Immediate_and_Mid_Term_Mass_Trauma_Intervention_Empirical_Evidence

Holiday, R. (2014). The Obstacle is the Way: The timeless art of turning trials into triumph. London: Penguin.

Hului, P. (2019a). Having a Taste of Adan Rice from the Krayan Highlands. Krago Mag Apr 22, 2019 Retrieved July 25, 2020 from https://kajomag.com/having-a-taste-of-adan-rice-from-the-krayan-highlands/

Hului, P. (2019b). The Legend of How Salt Springs Were Discovered in the Krayan Highlands. Krago Mag Sep 11, 2019 Retrieved July 25, 2020 from https://kajomag.com/the-legend-of-how-salt-springs-were-discovered-in krayan-highlands/

Hunt, E.J.F., Wessely, S. Jones, N., Rona, R.J. & Greenberg, N., (2014). The Mental Health of the U.K. Armed Forces: Where fact meets fiction. European Journal of Psychotrauma.14 Aug, 2014, 5.

Indigenous works. (n.d.) Resources. Retrieved December 31, 2020 from https://indigenousworks.ca/en/resources/articles-reports/fire-and-dream

Ingram, D. J. (2015). Spectacular Helmeted Hornbill could be wiped out by Chinese Demand for Avian Ivory. The Conversation. Retrieved July 2, 2020 from https://theconversation.com/spectacular-helmeted-hornbill-could-be-wiped-out-by-chinese-demand-for-avian-ivory-50349

Inscape. (2017). Business Agility: Strategic Planning vs Strategic Thinking (4 Jan, 2017) Retrieved June 4, 2020 from https://www.inscapeconsulting.com/2020/03/business-agility-strategic-planning-vs-strategic-thinking/

Jackson, B.H. (2011). Finding Your Flow: How to identify your flow assets and liabilities-the keys to peak performance every day. Highland Utah: The Institute of Applied Human Excellence

Jelinek, M. &Litterer. (1995). Toward Entrepreneurial Organizations. Entrepreneurship Theory and Practice. 19 (3), 137-169

Jones, C. (2020). How the World's Smelliest Fruit Could Power Your Phone. BBC News Energy 26 July, 2020 Retrieved July 26, 2020 from https://www.bbc.com/future/article/20200724-the-battery-made-from-diamonds-that-could-last-1000-years

Joomla! (2020). Frogs of Borneo. Retrieved June 25, 2020 from http://frogsofborneo.org/microhylidae/246-microhylidae/kalophrynus/pleurostigma-meizon

Kanyi, E., Strategic Thinking vs Strategic Planning. Oct 18, 2011, http://sbs.strath- more.edu/blog/2011/09/09/146/

Kahneman, D., & Tversky, A. (1979). Prospect theory: An analysis of decision under risk. Econometrica, 47, 263-291

Kimberly, J.R. & Miles, R.H. (1980). The Organizational Lifecycle; Issues in the creation, transformation and decline of organizations. San Francisco: Jossey-Bass.

Koepcke, J. (2012). How I Survived a Plane Crash BBC News 24 March, 2020 Retrieved July 2, 2020 from https://www.bbc.com/news/magazine-17476615

Koestner, R.J. (2008). Lost Person Behavior:A search and rescue guide on where to look for land, air and water. Charlottesville, VA: DBS Productions.

Kopenawa, D. (2020). Survival International Indigenous skills of tribal peoples. London: Survival International. Retrieved June 4, 2020 from https://www.survivalinternational.org/galleries/ingenious

Kotter, J.P. (1996). Leading Change. Boston: Harvard Business School Press.

Lal, J.J. (2003). Sago Palm. in Encyclopedia of Food Sciences and Nutrition (Second Edition), Retrieved May 20, 2020 from https://www.sciencedirect.com/topics/agricultural-and-biological-sciences/sago-palm

Langer, E.J. (1989). Mindfulness. Reading PA: Addison-Wesley.

Langub, J. (2012). Krayan Highland Salt in Central Borneo: Its uses and significance. Borneo Research Bulletin Vol. 43 pp 186-204. Institute of East Asian Studies Universiti Malaysia Sarawak Kota Samarahan, Sarawak Malaysia Retrieved July 25, 2020 from

Leach, J. (2011). Survival Psychology: The won't to live. The Psychologist. Jan 2011 Vol. 24 (pp 26-29) https://thepsychologist.bps.org.uk/volume-24/edition-1/survival-psychology-wont-live Retrieved July 26, 2020 from https://www.questia.com/library/journal/1G1-336176491/krayan-highland-salt-in-central-borneo-its-uses-and

Leaver, A.M., Yang, H., Siddarth, P., Vlasova, R.M., Krause, B., St Cyr, N., Narr, K.L.& Lauretsky, H. (2018). Resilience and Amygdala Function in Older Healthy and Depressed Adults. J Affect Disord. 2018 Sep: 237:27-34.doi: 10.1016/j.jad.2018.04.109. Epub 2018 Apr 25. Retrieved June 6, 2020 from https://pubmed.ncbi.nlm.nih.gov/29754022/

Leider, R.J. (1997). The Power of Purpose: Creating meaning in your life and work. San Francisco: Berrett-Koehler.

Lewin, K. (1951). Field theory in Social Science: Selected theoretical Papers. (Ed. Dorwin Cartwright) New York: Harper.

Look, J. (2017). Thomas Wolfe was Right: You can't go home again. Forbes Sep 24, 2017 Retrieved January 2, 2020 from https://www.forbes.com/sites/nextavenue/2017/09/24/thomas-wolfe-was-right-you-cant-go-home-again/?sh=704d602ee847

Lost. (2020). Lexico by Oxford Online Dictionary. Retrieved December 17, 2020 from https://www.lexico.com/en/definition/lost

Lovitt, B. (2016). Death by Selfie:11 Disturbing stories of social media pics gone wrong. Rolling stone July 14, 2006 Retrieved July 30, 2020 from https://www.rollingstone.com/culture/culture-lists/death-by-selfie-11-disturbing-stories-of-social-media-pics-gone-wrong-15091/selfie-stick-lightning-rod-30043/

Margerison, C. (1987). Conversational Control Skills. San Francisco: Berrett-Koehler.

Min J. A., Jung Y. E., Kim D. J., Yim H. W., Kim J. J., Kim T. S., et al. (2012). Characteristics associated with low resilience in patients with depression and/or anxiety disorders. Qual. Life Res. [Epub ahead of print]. 10.1007/s11136-012-0153-3

Mink, O.G., Owen, K.Q., & Mink, B.P. (1993). Developing High-Performance People: The Art of Coaching. Cambridge, MA: Perseus Books.

McEwan, B.S. & Morrison, J.H. (2013). Brain On Stress: Vulnerability and plasticity of the Prefrontal Cortex over the life course. Neuron. 2013 Jul 10: 79 (1) 16-29 Retrieved June 6, 2020 from doi: 10.1016/j.neuron.2013.06.028https://www.ncbi.nlm.nih.gov/pmc/articles/PMC3753223/

McRae K., Ochsner K. N., Mauss I. B., Gabrieli J. D., Gross J. J. (2008). Gender differences in emotion regulation: an fMRI study of cognitive reappraisal. Group Process. Intergr. Relat. *11*, 143–162

Morgan, G. (1988). Riding the Waves of Change: Developing managerial competencies for a turbulent world. San Francisco: Jossey-Bass.

Makussara, M. (2020). Personal Communications. June 4, 2020.

Nisbett, R., Chua, H.F. & Boland, J.E. (2005). Cultural Variation in Eye Movement During Scene Perception. Proceedings of the National Academy of Sciences 102 (35): 12629-33 September 2005 Retrieved 30 July, 30, 2020 from https://www.researchgate.net/publication/7644828_Cultural_variation_in_eye_movement_during_scene_perception

NTSB. (1995). Factual report: Aviation. LAX95FA046. National Transportation Safety Board.

Nuwer, R. (2014). Smithsonian News. Retrieved December 17, 2020 from https://www.smithsonianmag.com/smart-news/borneo-has-lost-30-percent-its-forest-cover

O'Hanlon, R. (1987). Into the Heart of Borneo. New York: Vintage Departures.

Ozbay F., Fitterling H., Charney D., Southwick S. (2008). Social support and resilience to stress across the life span: A neurobiologic framework. Curr. Psychiatry Rep. *10*, 304–310 Retrieved July 23, 2020 from doi: 10.1007/s11920-008-0049-7.

Palmer, W. (1999). The Intuitive Body: Aikido as a Clairsentient practice. Berkeley, CA: North Atlantic Books.

Parrado, N. & Rause, V. (2006). Miracle in the Andes: 72 days on the mountain and my long trek home. New York: Crown.

Pelton, R.Y. (2007). The World's Most Dangerous Places. New York, New York: Harper Collins.

Perrow, C. (2003). Disaster Prevention and Mitigation. Yale Sociology Working Paper, New Haven CT: Yale University.

Phillips, D. (2013). FSG, Reimagining Social Change. The Story of Outward Bound and Why Experiential Education Matters. Jan 23, 2013 Retrieved January 2, 2021 from https://www.fsg.org/blog/story-outward-bound-and-why-experiential-education-matters.

Picheta, R. & Pleiten, F., (2020). A suspect package sent six people to the hospital and caused an evacuation—its contents turned out to be some very smelly fruit. CNN June 22, 2020 Retrieved June 22, 2020 from https://www.cnn.com/2020/06/22/europe/durian-germany-evacuation-scli-intl-grm/index.html

Plutniak, S. Ferri, J., Oktaviana, A.A., Sugiyanto, B., Sarei, J., Fauzi, R., Simanjuntak, T., Guerreiro, A., Grenet, M. & Ricaut, F.X., (2014). Human Occupation of the Mangkalihat Karstic Area: Rock art and settlement history in East Kalimantan. The Free Library. Jan 2014 Retrieved June 29, 2020 from https://www.thefreelibrary.com/Human+occupation+of+the+Mangkalihat+Karstic+area%3a+rock+art+and...-a0420435235

Powell, D.W. (2015). How Not to Lose your Bass in Business: Business is like Fishing. New York: DocUMeantPublishing.

Puri, R.K., (2005). Deadly Dances in the Borneo Rainforest: Hunting knowledge of the Penan Benalui. Leiden: KITLV Press.

Rahnema, A. & Murphy, T. (2020). The Adaptable Organization: Harnessing a networked enterprise of Human Resilience. Deloitte Development Retrieved July 2, 2020 from https://www2.deloitte.com/content/dam/Deloitte/global/Documents/HumanCapital/adaptable-organization.pdf

Richards, R. & McEwan, M. (1989). The survival factor. Tunbridge Wells: DJ Costello.

Robson, D. (2017). How the East and West Think in Profoundly Different Ways: Psychologists are uncovering the surprising influence of geography on our reasoning, behavior, and sense of self. Retrieved July 2, 2020 from https://www.bbc.com/future/article/20170118-how-east-and-west-think-in-profoundly-different-ways

Robson, D. (2020). The Astonishing Vision and Focus of Namibia's Nomads. 26 June, 2020 Retrieved December 17, 2020 from https://

www.bbc.com/future/article/20170306-the-astonishing-focus-of-na-mibias-nomads

Rotter, J. B. (1966). Generalized expectancies for internal versus external control of reinforcement. Psychological monographs: General and applied, 80 (1), 1.

Rutherford, J.R. (2011). The Littlest Green Beret: On self-reliant leadership. Saxonburg, PA: Pylon Publishing.

Sarrionandia, A., Ramos-Diaz, E. & Fernandez-Lasarte, O. (2018). Resilience as a Mediator of Emotional Intelligence and Perceived Stress: A Cross-Country Study. Frontiers of Psychology 21 Dec 2018 Retrieved July 17, 2020 from https://www.frontiersin.org/articles/10.3389/fpsyg.2018.02653/full

Schlossberg N. (1989). Overwhelmed: Coping with Life's Ups and Downs. New York: The Free Press. in Gebelein, S.H., Lee, D.G. & Sloan, E.B. (Eds.) The Executive Handbook: Development suggestions for today's executives. 6th Ed. 2001, Minneapolis: Personnel Decisions International.

Schneider, T.R., Lyons, J.B. & Khazon, S., (2013). Emotional Intelligence and Resilience. Personality and Individual Differences. Volume 55, Issue 8 Nov 2013 Pages 909-914 Retrieved July 17, 2020 from https://www.sciencedirect.com/science/article/abs/pii/S0191886913007460

Schwartz, T. & McCarthy, C. (2007). In Manage Your Energy Not Your Time. Boston: HBR Press. pp. 61-79.

Seligman, M.E.P. (2006). Learned Optimism: How to change your mind and your life. New York: Knopf-Doubleday.

Sherwood, B., (2009). The Survivor's Club: The secrets and science that could save your life. CD New York: Hachette Audio.

Siebert, A. (1996). The Survivor Personality. New York: Penguin Putnam.

Singer, T. (2012). The Perfect Amount of Stress: Stress is a killer. How can you tell the good from the bad, and too little from too much? Psychology Today. March 13, 2012 Retrieved December 12, 2020 from https://www.psychologtoday.com/us/articles/201203/the-perfect-amount-stress

Southwick S. M., Vythilingam M., Charney D. S. (2005). The psychobiology of depression and resilience to stress: Implications for prevention and treatment. Annual Review of Clinical Psychology *1*, 255–291

Retrieved July 23, 2020 from 10.1146/annurev.clinpsy.https://pubmed.
ncbi.nlm.nih.gov/17716089/

Southwick S. M. & Charney D. S. (2012). The science of resilience: implications for the prevention and treatment of depression. Science 338,
79–82 10.1126/science.1222942 Retrieved July 23, 2020 from https://
pubmed.ncbi.nlm.nih.gov/23042887/

Stewart D. E., Yuen T. (2011). A systematic review of resilience in the
physically ill. Psychosomatics 52, 199–209 10.1016/j.psym.2011.01.036
Retrieved July 23, 2020 from https://pubmed.ncbi.nlm.nih.
gov/21565591/

Susiarti, S. (1995). Knowledge and utilization of medicinal plant in
Apauping village and surrounding areas, Pujungan district, East
Kalimantan (Indonesia)1995.Seminar dan Lokakarya Nasional
Etnobotani Retrieved May 20, 2020 from https://agris.fao.org/agris-
search/search.do?recordID=ID1997000472

Swaminathan, N. (2008). Why Does the Brain Need So Much Power?:
New study shows why the brain drains so much of the body's energy.
Scientific American. April 29, 2008. Retrieved July 5, 2020 from
https://www.scientificamerican.com/article/why-does-the-brain-
need-s/

Swenson, R.A. (1992). Margin: Restoring Emotional, Physical, Financial,
and Time Reserves to Overloaded Lives. Colorado Springs: Nav Press.

Thabet, A.A.M. (2017). Trauma, Mental Health, Coping, Resilience:
Post Traumatic Growth (PG) Palestinian experience. JOJ Nurs-
ing and Healthcare. Vol. 2 Issue 2 June 2017. Juniper Publishers.
Retrieved June 6, 2020 from https://juniperpublishers.com/jojnhc/
pdf/JOJNHC.MS.ID.555583.pdf

Thompson R. W., Arnkoff D. B., Glass C. R. (2011). Conceptualizing
mindfulness and acceptance as components of psychological resilience to trauma. Trauma. Violence Abuse 12, 220–235 10.1177/152
4838011416375 Retrieved July 23, 2020 from http://citeseerx.ist.psu.
edu/viewdoc/download?doi=10.1.1.1029.497&rep=rep1&type=pdf

Thompson, N. & Thomspon, S. (2015). The Social Work Companion. 2nd
Ed. London: Red Globe.

Tillema H.F. (1989). A Journey Among the Peoples of Central Borneo in
Word and Picture. New York: Oxford University Press.

Tsai J., Harpaz-Rotem I., Pietrzak R. H., Southwick S. M. (2012). The role of coping, resilience, and social support in mediating the relation between PTSD and social functioning in veterans returning from Iraq and Afghanistan. Psychiatry 75, 135–149 10.1521/psyc.2012.75.2.1 Retrieved July 23, 2020 from https://pubmed.ncbi.nlm.nih.gov/22642433/

Vaill, P.B. (1996). Learning as a Way of Being: Strategies for survival in a world of permanent whitewater. San Francisco: Jossey-Bass.

Vasel, K. (2020). Google will give every employee $1,000 to WFH. Its head of wellness explains why. CNN Business June 4, 2020, Retrieved June 4, 2020 from https://www.cnn.com/2020/06/04/success/google-wellness/index.html

Walker, M. (2011). Adventure in Everything: How the five elements of adventure create a life of authenticity, purpose and inspiration. Carlsbad, CA: Hay House.

Walters, B.B., McCay, B.J., West, P.& Lees, S. (2008). Against the Grain: The Vayda Tradition in Human Ecology and Ecological Anthropology. Walnut, CA: Altamira Press.

Warner L. M., Schwarzer R., Schuz B., Wurm S., Tesch-Romer C. (2012). Health-specific optimism mediates between objective and perceived physical functioning in older adults. J. Behav. Med. *35*, 400–406 10.1007/s10865-011-9368-y Retrieved July 23, 2020 from https://pubmed.ncbi.nlm.nih.gov/21720826/

Watkins, M. (2003). The First 90 days: Critical strategies for new leaders at all levels. Boston, MA: Harvard Business School Press.

Weick, K.E. & Sutcliffe, K.M. (2001). Managing the Unexpected: Assuring high performance in an age of complexity. Ann Arbor, MI: University of Michigan Press.

Weick, K.E. (1993). The collapse of sensemaking in organizations: the Mann Gulch disaster. Administrative Science Quarterly 38: 628-652. (1995) Sensemaking in Organizations. Thousand Oaks, CA: Sage

Weick, K.E. (1995). Sensemaking in Organizations. Thousand Oaks, CA: Sage.

Weisbord, M.R. (1976). Organizational Diagnosis: Six places to look for trouble with or without a theory. Group and Organization Studies 1, 4 (Dec 1976): 430-447

Wolvin, A.D. & Coakley, C.G. (1996). *Listening (5th ed.)* New York, N.Y.: McGraw-Hill.

Woodman, J. (n.d.). Goodreads. Retrieved from Retrieved December 17, 2020 from https://www.goodreads.com/quotes/4101436-life-is-a-repeated-cycle-of-getting-lost-and-then

World Wildlife Fund. (2011). Eco-tourism-One of the building blocks for eco-tourism in the HOB. Retrieved June 4, 2020 from https://wwf.panda.org/?202818/Eco-tourism--one-of-the-building-blocks-for-a-green-Economy-in-the-HoB).

World Wildlife Fund. (n.d.). The Human Heart of Borneo. Retrieved July 16th, 2020 from https://wwf.panda.org/knowledge_hub/where_we_work/borneo_forests/about_borneo_forests/people/

Zahorka, H. (2004). Ein mechanisches Blasrohr verschiesst GiRpfeile. Hessen Jager 23/2:10. DLW.

Zahorka, H. (2006). Blowpipe dart poison in Borneo and the secret of its production: the latex of Antiaris toxicara; the poison- making procedure; the heat-sensitive main toxic chemical compound, and the lethal effect of the poison. Borneo Research Bulletin January 1, 2006. Retrieved July 12, 2020 from http://www.thefreelibrary.com/_/print/PrintArticle.aspx?id=166350047

Zhang, M. (2014). The Founder Of FedEx Saved The Company From Bankruptcy With His Blackjack Winnings. Business Insider Jul 16, 2014. Retrieved May 7, 2020 from https://www.businessinsider.com/fedex-savedfrom-bankruptcy-with-blackjack-winnings-2014

Acknowledgements

We would like to express our deep appreciation to the people who made our travels through Indonesia such a deep and meaningful experience.

Thank you to the people of the towns of Long Layu and Apauping who searched for us after we were delayed, sent food out with the search parties, and invited us into their villages with such warmth, grace and hospitality before and after our travels in the jungle.

Thank you to the Indonesian military, officers and soldiers, and to the village chiefs who organized search parties so efficiently and professionally.

Thank you to my dear friend Barbara for being so supportive of all my adventures and for all your endless hours of editing and feedback that helped shape my scattered thoughts into a book.

About the Author

Steve Camkin is an author, adventurer, executive coach, speaker, facilitator and organizational consultant.

As an author...Steve wrote the Amazon International Best Seller *High Altitude Leadership: Small steps to get you to the top of big mountains.* His next book *Whitewater Leadership* will be released in early 2022.

As an adventurer...Steve climbed the Seven Summits, led and participated in expeditions on 7 continents including a solo 550-mile winter mountain biking trip down the frozen Yukon River in Alaska. As a former Chief Instructor for Outward Bound Steve led multi-sports expeditions of up to 42 days in length.

As an international executive coach...Steve currently supports clients from locations as diverse as Pakistan, Turkey, Egypt, Thailand and Russia with leadership development and executive presentation skills.

As a speaker...Steve brings to his audiences a unique, engaging and adventurous perspective to leadership, team and organizational development through creative metaphors and storytelling.

As a facilitator and organizational consultant...Steve has, for more than 25 years, worked in 18 countries with clients such as BP, Barclays, Amalgamated Banks of South Africa, Honeywell, Home Depot, Oracle, Nestle, the New Zealand Department of Maori Affairs, PayPal, Pepsi, Salesforce and the Saudi Government.

After growing up in Australia and New Zealand he now lives in Boise, Idaho where he skies, bikes, kayaks, backpacks and serves as a member of Idaho's Mountain Search and Rescue Team.

Steve can be reached at www.DrSteveCamkin.com

Made in the USA
Columbia, SC
23 November 2021

49485918R00147